The Future of the Parish System

The Future of the Parish System

Shaping the Church of England for the twenty-first century

Edited by Steven Croft

CHURCH HOUSE
PUBLISHING

Church House Publishing
Church House
Great Smith Street
London SW1P 3NZ

Tel: 020 7898 1451
Fax: 020 7898 1449

ISBN-13 978-0-7151-4034-5
ISBN-10 0 7151 4034 5

Published 2006 by Church House Publishing

*The opinions expressed in this book are those of the authors and
do not necessarily reflect the official policy of the General Synod or
The Archbishops' Council of the Church of England.*

Cover design by S2 design and advertising

Typeset in Rotis Semi Sans by RefineCatch Limited, Bungay, Suffolk

Printed in England by MPG Books Ltd, Bodmin, Cornwall

Contents

Contents

Introduction

It was the best of times . . . it was the worst of times.
Charles Dickens, *A Tale of Two Cities*

The Church of England is passing through a time of significant change and great opportunity. The changes sometimes bring discomfort and some dangers to our common life. However, they are also generating immense creativity and the possibility of new things.

Many of the changes are external to the Church itself: they are part of the world in which we live. Our society is becoming more diverse; patterns of family life and work are changing; choice is a greater feature of our world; new technologies affect the way we live. Changes in society bring the need for new reflection on what the Church believes and teaches.

For many years, church attendance has been in decline. We may be witnessing the first signs that this decline may be coming to an end. Certainly, there is growth in many individual congregations and some dioceses. There are many indications that people are interested again in spirituality even if they do not always connect that interest with the churches.

Over the last generation, the Church of England has had to navigate a pathway through all of this change at a national level – in its dioceses and in its local parishes. We have had to learn many lessons. We have made mistakes (though not all of us would agree on what they are). As a Church, we have lost at least some of our arrogance and self-assurance in that process. We have learned lessons from Christians in different parts of the world and have adapted those lessons to our context. We have looked back to Scripture and to our tradition and quarried fresh resources for ministry and mission. But there is still some way to go.

As I look at the Church of England at the present time, I see a Church in which there is a great deal of life and hope; a Church at its best marked by humility, perseverance, courage and generosity; a Church which holds together (albeit, sometimes, with great difficulty) Christians with very different views; a Church committed to sharing in God's mission in our own society and around the world; a church that is willing to be changed; a Church committed not to blowing its own trumpet but to singing the Lord's song in a stranger land.

Yet I also see a Church that is beset by an endemic anxiety about the future, which breaks to the surface in a range of debates. That anxiety is fed by an almost continual blizzard of prophecies of doom and decline. They come within, from those who see forecasts of decline as a lever for change and who do not realize that their careless predictions sap hope and energy. They come from without, from those who would like nothing better than to reduce the influence of the churches in our national life.

As the Church of England, we need to make wise decisions in order to shape our future. Those decisions are needed in parishes, clusters and deaneries; they are needed in dioceses and in national Church life. They are needed with some urgency. But, anxiety never produces the kind of wisdom that is required. It can too easily create a climate in which we climb on bandwagons, adopt simplistic solutions, buy into the latest franchise, which guarantees success, bury our heads in the sand or veer this way and that at the mercy of every wind of change.

Our decisions need to be guided, tested and shaped by Scripture and our long tradition. In a storm a boat needs its keel perhaps more than its rudder. Our decisions need to be informed also by the realities of the world in which we find ourselves. The aim of this book is to provide not answers but resources to inform this great process of reflection, learning and action to which we are called by God in our generation.

As authors we have tried to draw out some basic principles from a range of different disciplines and perspectives that shed light on the times we are living in and the directions we may be called to take.

You won't find in these pages a blueprint for the future. You won't find a group of authors who entirely agree with each other, although we are singing broadly from the same hymn sheet: it is often through difference and dialogue that true wisdom emerges. You may not even find, from your perspective, a 'balanced' book in terms of the different traditions and perspectives represented or the conclusions it reaches.

Inevitably, the choice of contributors was subjective: in consultation with the publishers, I invited contributions from people who I believe have important things to say from a range of perspectives to inform and help shape the future. Several of the contributors were included because their writing, in different forms, has influenced my own thinking in uncomfortable ways. This is not a working party assembled to produce a report but a group of scholars, observers, ministers and disciples each bringing a different perspective.

Undergirding those different perspectives, however, there are two common principles. The first is a perspective of hope for the Church and the conviction that our hope is not based on evidence or trends or what we observe around us but is rooted in God's grace and mercy and faithfulness. Hope is a theological virtue. We live in the time of the resurrection of the Son of God. The life of God's Spirit flows still in (often clogged) arteries of God's Church. It is primarily because of the faithfulness of God, Father, Son and Holy Spirit, that we expect to see continual new life flowering in the life of the Church of England and our sister churches. The first calling of our Church is to respond to the grace and generosity of God in worship, thanksgiving and prayer.

The second principle is a conviction that, in order to share in the mission of God in our own generation, we are called to develop our existing churches and communities with their own traditions but we are also called to encourage and begin fresh expressions of church. The Archbishop of Canterbury coined the phrase 'mixed economy church' while he was still a bishop in Wales. It catches well this 'both-and' approach to our church life which is being taken forward with commitment and love in many different dioceses and ecumenically. This thinking is developed further in the watershed report, *Mission-shaped Church*, published in 2004. Some of the essays in this book refer, and will be helpful, to both sides of this mixed economy: parish churches seeking to be mission-shaped and fresh expressions of church bearing witness to God's love in new ways and new communities. Others focus on one or other aspect of the future life of Christian communities within the Church of England.

As authors, we have tried to avoid using a range of (we believe) rather tired dichotomies and setting them against each other: maintenance or mission; social action or evangelism; fresh expressions of church or the traditional parish structures. All of these different elements are needed in the future shape of diocesan and parish life. We have not bound ourselves to agree on every point but nor have we sought to disagree deliberately either. We share a perspective that the future of the Church of England will need to be worked out in an ecumenical partnership with our sister churches but we have written with a specifically Anglican vocabulary and context in mind.

The 'shape' of the book is, I hope, clear from the table of contents. The opening chapters give a perspective on the problems and changes we face from the viewpoint of what is happening in our wider society, from history and from the discipline of psychology. Part Two aims to offer some theological resources for our thinking on church, on ministry and mission. Part Three attempts to work on ways forward in the light of this reflection in a range of different contexts. Each essay is designed to be read independently (and so the book can be read in any order) but we believe each makes a contribution to an emerging picture.

We hope that the book will be useful to ministers and congregations, those preparing for recognized ministries and to all who share in the life and governance of the Church of England. We have a particular hope that it might stimulate discussion among those who work together in a range of different ministry contexts. We are aware of much that we haven't included in the book (and no doubt that will be pointed out in due course). We make no apology for keeping mission central to our reflection. We hope that some of the essays here will be able speak to those in other denominations who are wrestling with similar questions.

I would like to record my thanks to the authors who have responded to difficult briefs to write (and to editorial suggestions) with patience and care. A book such as this can only be one contribution to the Church of England's ongoing reflection on the questions we face. We hope and pray that it will contribute to the development of wisdom and reflection that is needed as we navigate through times of such opportunity and grace.

Steven Croft
February 2006

PART ONE:
UNDERSTANDING OUR CONTEXT

1

Many rooms in my Father's house: The changing identity of the English parish church[1]

Martyn Percy

Martyn Percy is Principal of Ripon College Cuddesdon. In this opening chapter in this first section of the book, he offers the perspective of history on the changing nature and identity of the parish church. He argues that we need to set our present context against the longer perspective of the past and not give in to despair.

Some years ago I was asked to fill in a questionnaire for a school survey run by some children. The question was this: 'What is the Church?' My answer was as follows:

> Partly a building

> Partly people

> Partly an ideal

> Partly complete

The idea of partiality to describe the church is fascinating, especially when compared to the kingdom of God that might be glimpsed on the other side: 'the heavenly city, coming down like a bride, complete . . .', or, 'in my father's house there are many rooms . . .'; so no need for extensions, then. It is enough; it is finished. But, as though we need reminding, we as a people are not; we remain deficient and incomplete. And neither is our church ever the finished product. Yet God accepts us, and continually beckons us to his house – the heavenly place where there is room for all.

Speaking of room for all, we remember too, that this is the vision behind what it means to be a parish church. The word 'parish' is never used in the New Testament, but it is, interestingly, an ancient Greek word, which literally means 'those outside the house': not the insiders, but the outsiders. The Greeks used it to refer to the areas of a city where the non-citizens lived – those with few rights, who were non-Greeks, and therefore excluded. So a parish church, in an ideal world, is not an exclusive place, but an inclusive place for the local stranger; for those who don't know the way, the truth and the life; for those who don't know they have a place in the heart of God, and who are ignorant of their room reservation in heaven. It is the inside place for the outsider; the only club that exists for non-members, as William Temple once quipped.

Set alongside this theological vision is the realization that the English parish church, as Sara Savage argues in the next chapter, is part and parcel of the cultural furniture of the nation. To some it is a place of denominational worship; for others it is the natural focus of the community; for still others, a place of Christian *witness* within a community.

These idealist descriptions of the parish church all have their merit. But what does it mean to talk about a parish church today?

The question is a timely one when one considers the various subtle and inimical forces that appear to have eroded the identity of the concept. Religious pluralism has been a feature of the landscape of English religion since the Reformation; a parish church is no longer the sole focus for the religious rituals of its people, nor for their spiritual aspirations. Changes in population and in churchgoing habits have also left their mark.

Yet there have been other periods when parochial sustainability and viability seemed threatened. For example, Winchester could once claim to be the most over-churched city in England, with, in the twelfth century, a cathedral, two monasteries and at least 57 churches for a population serving no more than 8,000 people; that is one parish church for every 130 people. What did 8,000 people *do* with 57 churches and a cathedral? It would appear that these churches were made up of congregations serving relatively small communities. By 1535, the number of parish churches in Winchester had fallen to just 13 – a quarter of the number for the twelfth century.

I will reflect on the identity of the English parish church and explore some of the ways in which the pressures it now faces are particular and specious. In order to do this, it will first be necessary to 'de-bunk' the myth of secularization. Most sociologists of religion no longer accept that modernity necessarily ushers in a less religious era. Religion in the modern world does not suffer as one might immediately suppose; granted, it mutates, is squeezed into new shapes, and patterns of religious affinity and belonging are certainly altering. But, with the onset of modernity, the world has *not* become a less religious place. People continue to possess and express what we scholars of religion variously call 'innate', 'folk' or 'common' spirituality, or 'vernacular religion'.

The concept of the parish church has some apparent ambiguities: the very idea of a parish church can be said, to some extent, to be a bit of an accident. The Saxon age is the first phase in the development of the concept. Minster churches – hundreds were dotted around England – devolved spiritual responsibility to smaller units – 'parish churches' – that were charged with the task of ministering to local communities. A community now defined as a parish was an economically viable community that could not only pay its secular taxes, but could also afford its spiritual duties. Even then, a system of tithing existed to support the ministry and fabric of the church, and that system survived well into the nineteenth century.

In short, the viability of a church was deeply connected to the viability of a community; church and parish lived in a relation of intra-dependence. Payment of fees to the church meant that the poor were cared for, that sacramental ministry was provided, the dead were buried honourably, and that the moral welfare of the community was generally catered for. The church needed a parish; and the parish needed its church. But this relationship began to bifurcate even before the Reformation, and so the waning and mutating identity of a parish church has (at least initially) nothing to do with secularization. With these observations in mind, the questions that this chapter is concerned with are as follows. With the collapse of parochial identity in contemporary English culture (a process that appears to pre-date the Reformation), what can a parish church offer to its environment and to its people? And to what extent can a space such as a parish church be meaningfully spoken of when many people have lost their conscious sense of belonging to a parochial space?

The myth of secular England: A brief sketch

One of the great paradoxes of late modernity is that, almost more than any other group, churches believe in the steady decrease of public faith. During the last half of the twentieth century, it has been popular to believe in a new credo: secularization. Promoted by a few busy sociologists in league with disenchanted voices in the media, the belief is simple enough. The more advanced or modern society becomes, the less it looks to the spiritual and the religious. Therefore, church attendance declines, and the once golden age of Christendom, at least in the West, is coming to its end. The thesis appears to be supported by statistics; fewer people go to church than, say, 100 years ago, so the long-term prognosis seems to be correct.

As with most things, the truth is not nearly so simple. We now know enough about church-going habits to make a more sober, less bleak judgement about the parish church. It doesn't take a mathematical genius to figure out that if churchgoers who once went 52 times a year (and on high days and holy days) now only go 47 times a year (allowing for vacations), this leads to a 10 per cent drop in attendance. But there are not 10 per cent fewer people attending church; what has changed is the performance of the worshippers. It may be the case that more people come to church less frequently, and that *regular* churchgoing is in decline, but the appetite for occasional church attendance seems undiminished. Granted, less people belong, formally, to a Christian denomination when compared to the inter-war or Victorian periods. But most forms of association have declined steeply since those days. Associational disconnection is an endemic feature of modern life, but, ironically, churches are holding up far better than many of their secular counterparts.

For example, today there are fewer Scouts and Guides; Trade Union membership has waned; and there are now fewer members of the Conservative Party than there are Methodists. Bodies such as the Freemasons, Round Table, Townswomen's Guilds and Women's Institutes have noted steep declines in membership; but the Mothers' Union has held out rather well by comparison. Recreationally, there are fewer people in our cinemas and football grounds than seventy years ago – yet no one can say these activities are in decline. Indeed, it is a sobering thought that in so-called secular Britain, there are still more people turning to God each weekend at a church than out watching a game of football.

Another problem with secularization is that, after sociologists and the media, those who believe in this thesis most passionately are the churches themselves. Many, if not most, have bought the idea that modernity leads to the gradual and incremental loss of faith. Correspondingly, various interest groups emerge, hoping to make some capital out of the perceived crisis. Liberals propose stripping the faith to its bare essentials in order to make religion more credible. Evangelicals also strip the faith to its essentials, and promote 'the basics' of religion through courses like *Alpha*. But most

Christians (though it is never easy to say *who* these people are, nor exactly what their faith consists of) who are in the middle ground are rather bewildered by these approaches to faith and society. For in their day-to-day Christian existence, no matter how intense or nominal, they do not encounter a 'secular' world at all, but, rather, one in which spirituality, religion and questions of faith remain public and widespread. In short, they do not believe in the modern 'disease' of secularization, and consequently, they are un-persuaded by those groups that seek to promote their panaceas.

But surely there is some truth in the idea that fewer people are turning to official or mainstream religion? Yes and no. To a large extent, it depends on what periods in history are being compared to the present. For example, the Victorian period saw a revival of religion and religious attendance that lasted for about 40 years. Yet the beginnings of the eighteenth and nineteenth centuries were eras that were very much the opposite of this: church attendance was, on the whole, derisory.

The medieval and Reformation periods are often characterized as ages of great faith. However, the general scale of apathy and antipathy should not be underestimated. The eleventh-century monk, William of Malmesbury complained that the aristocracy rarely attended mass, while the very poor – then as now – hardly attended church at all. There have been very few periods in English history when everyone went to church or Sunday school, knew right from wrong, and absolutely hung on every word their parish priest uttered. Detailed readings of parochial records from almost any age can illustrate the pragmatic, amateurish nature of 'official' English religion.

The Archdiaconal Visitation of 1578 for Bedfordshire[2] shows its parish churches apparently in a poor state of repair, with theft of lead and timber being relatively commonplace. Meanwhile, the clergy appear to be mostly absent from their churches, squashing the myth that every parish was (until recently) well served by its own parish priest. In many cases churches in Bedfordshire had not seen a priest for months or even years, and the concerns of the churchwardens are similar to the concerns expressed by the churchwardens of the twenty-first century: 'When will we get our next vicar, bishop?' and 'What is to be done about the state of our church?' The agenda for the parish church is as old as the hills: without staffing and proper maintenance, there is a fear for the identity and viability of the community as a whole.

This haphazard, semi-secular, quiet (but occasionally rowdy and irreverent) English Christianity continues well into successive centuries. James Woodforde's *Diary of a Country Parson* provides an invaluable window into the life of the clergy and the state of English Christianity in the eighteenth century. Whatever secularization is, it is not obviously a product of the Industrial Revolution. Woodforde clearly thinks it is reasonably good to have 'two rails' (or 30 communicants) at Christmas or Easter, from 360 parishioners. Such figures would be low by today's standards in some rural communities. Woodforde tells us that the only time his church is ever full is when a member of the royal family is ill, or when there is a war on. Generally, the context of his ministry is one where he baptizes, marries and buries the people of his parish, but the week-by-week Sunday attendance is not something that would get many ministers into a frenzy of excitement. But Woodforde is not bothered by this – not because he is especially lazy – but because the *totality* of his contact with his parish constitutes his ministry. He is *with* his people in all their trials and tribulations, not just his congregation. He is their man for all seasons; an incarnate presence in the midst of a community that waxes and wanes in its religious affections.

What needs to be stressed at the end of this short section is that the parish church and the ministry that issued from it was, generally speaking, greatly valued by the parish. However, that valuing did not necessarily translate into frequent and intense church attendance on the part of the masses. Mostly, it seems that the English have tended to *relate* to their parish churches in a variety of ways. This partly reflects a relationship of affection (sometimes grudging), of vicarious religion (of having others to believe in those things that one can't quite be so certain of – 'say one for me, padre', etc.), and of 'believing without belonging', to borrow phrases explored later by Grace Davie. Statistical surveys continually support the thesis that England is a place where the vast majority of the population continue to affirm their belief in God, but then proceed to do little about it. So church attendance figures remain stubbornly low. Yet this is not a modern malaise, but is rather a typical feature of many western societies down the ages. Granted, there have been periods of revival when church attendance has peaked. But the basic and innate disposition of the English is typical of western Europe – one of believing without belonging; of relating to the church, and valuing its presence and beliefs – yet without necessarily sharing them. Or, as the ageless witticism expresses it: 'I cannot consider myself to be a pillar of the Church, for I never go. But I am a buttress – in so far as I support it from the outside'.

The contemporary English parish church: An ambiguous identity?

With these brief reflections in mind, we now turn to the ambiguity of the parish church in contemporary English culture. What does it stand for? Whom does it serve? As many ministers of religion already know, the shape and content of parish ministry has altered radically over the last century. It is true that rates of church going were buoyant during the Victorian era, but the peaks and troughs of church attendance figures have nearly always depended as much upon cultural factors (for example, the shifting population from agrarian to industrial contexts, or in the case of the Billy Graham evangelistic campaigns of the post-war era, the shift from cities to a new suburbia) as they have on the intensity of engagement between a church and its parish.

Parish churches and their ministers throughout the nineteenth and twentieth centuries were, in effect, being forced to re-invent their connectedness to the parish. The obligation of tithing was withering, if not altogether defunct, which meant that the parish now had no necessary economic relationship with its church (besides which, other denominations had received legal recognition since 1689). The 'church-rate' that levied a tax on local people for the upkeep of the parish church was abolished by law in 1864, leading to the present anomalous situation, whereby the whole parish has access to the parish church for baptisms, weddings, funerals and other rites, but only members of the congregation are obliged to pay for the upkeep of the building. The experience of Victorian parochial ministry was one of more intense engagement as the parish and the church underwent rapid bifurcation, with the parish – as a space – ceasing to be recognized, except as a division of boroughs and civic authorities. Or, to put it another way, the increasing loss of the parish as a recognized 'place' that began in Victorian England – a product of industrialization, capitalism and early globalization – led to the parish church becoming a more intensely and exclusively spiritual space.

The continuing development of modernity has carried on changing the nature of locality. Air travel has led to a decline in passenger shipping, which has isolated many remote island communities. Thus, while for some the world is more compressed and globalized, for others it is increasingly lonely and fractious. Technology also reduces spatial distances – fax, email and video-phone – yet many still travel long distances just to collect water. The city may be alive and well, with everything 'within easy reach'; yet pensioners can still be living in bed-sits, their presence or absence going undetected for many months. In other words, the mobility of some, while destroying the identity of the 'local' for many, can equally leave many others depending even more heavily on their immediate environment and community for support.

But let us return to the relationship between the parish church and the parish locality. I noted at the beginning of this chapter that their identities had begun to undergo a process of bifurcation that can be dated from the Reformation, and in all probability well before that. For example, even from the early middle ages, it became increasingly difficult to order and police growing populations through the auspices of the local church. Courts of law, the rise of civic authorities and guilds, the need for better transport infrastructures and the like meant that many people looked beyond their immediate parochial boundaries for their livelihood. As we observed earlier, in small cities such as Winchester, what passed for 'parochial worship' was essentially congregational in character – a parish church may just have consisted of a few extended families worshipping together, and whatever sacramental ministry they could afford. In turn, this dynamic emerged afresh in the wake of the Reformation, when religious services could easily be said at home, presided over by the head of the house, and gathered around the word, and not sacramental worship – what we could identify as an early form of vernacular spirituality.

Furthermore, the economic ties that bound parishes to their parish churches were beginning to break down as commerce became increasingly cosmopolitan. As people became more mobile, the local mattered less and less. These trends, present long before the Renaissance, never mind the Reformation, could only increase during the Industrial Revolution.

Two areas are particularly significant: birth and death. Under the Saxon minster system, minster churches had once monopolized the rite of baptism; it was a sacrament undertaken by patronal churches, and the origin of the phrase 'mother church' partly lies in this fact. Other chapels and places of worship belonging to the minster rarely had fonts of their own. The fight to acquire the status of parish church was often about local autonomy and prestige against the interests of the minster. To be a parish church meant owning a font, and this in turn enabled the local church to be truly a community in its own right. Parish churches symbolized not only the presence of God in the midst of a community; they also made a powerful economic and social statement: this is a viable, living community that can support itself and support its God. A chapel said something different: we are dependent on another area for our welfare.

Baptism is only one half of the equation that allowed medieval chapels to make the uneasy transition to parish church. The other space that was required was a graveyard. Burials too allowed the community to 'own' their place of worship in a very particular way. The identity of a community could be entirely tied up with the location of the dead, and how the living memorialized them. The right to bury the dead signified that this 'place' was not transitory, but established. Not only was it a viable economic community, it was also a place that had a history and a right to a future.

I make these observations about parish churches in Saxon and medieval times because they were clearly important in maintaining a sense of place and in creating a kind of local identity, which was secular, sacred, religious, civic, local and catholic. Many parish churches today struggle to 'connect' with their locations in ways that are similar. In the case of births, baptismal rates have dropped steadily in England since the turn of the twentieth century, the trend accelerating with noticeable speed from the 1960s onwards. The response of the churches, interestingly, to this loss of *extensive* connection, has been to reify baptismal rites into a more *intensive* form of religious experience. Gone are the accommodating cultural customs of bygone eras in which the clergy baptized large numbers of children at times that were mainly convenient to families (that is, Sunday afternoons). Baptism ceases to be a social rite of passage – even the term 'Christening' is discouraged – and is replaced by something more definitive, with the baptismal service now more usually being situated within a normal Sunday morning service. The effect of this is hard to measure, but it would not be unfair to say that the parish church, in its loss of extensive connectedness with its own locality, has attempted to re-engage its disparate community by becoming more intense in its religious expression and by sharpening up its spiritual identity.

Another dynamic can be seen in relation to death. For most of the twentieth century, new churches that were built did not provide graveyards; gardens of rest for interred remains are a relatively late innovation. Death has moved, sociologically and culturally, from a commonplace event that was central to the life of all small communities and localities, to becoming something that is removed from the mainstream of society, and placed on its margins. Most deaths occur in hospitals, hospices or residential and nursing homes. The vast majority of funerals are conducted in anonymous crematoria that form no spatial, spiritual or social attachment with the bereaved. The memorialization of the dead – once the main point and function of a parish church – has been speedily eroded by the contemporary utilitarian forces that have tidied death up (in the name of clinical cleanliness) and swept it into the corners of modern life.

Predictably, the responses of the English parish churches to this have been pragmatic and pastoral. Remembrance Sunday refuses to die, long after its veterans have all been mourned. The festival of All Souls has undergone a renaissance in recent years, as churches have sought to restore the memorialization of death and the reality of bereavement, as well as speaking of resurrection, into a relationship with the communities they serve. The spaces and places for death may no longer exist in the way they once did, but there is always the compensation of calendrical ritual. And, as many churches discovered after 11 September 2001, or after the death of Princess Diana of Wales, an open church, in which to light a candle or say a prayer and sign a condolence book is still the first port of call for many people, and preferred to posting a message on the web.

The future of the parish church and its identity

Our reflections so far have hinted that the gradual bifurcation of the life of the parish church from the life of the parish community was a process that began prior to the Reformation, and has been as much about economic realities as it has about anything we might call secularization. We might also add that the gradual atomization of public space – a feature of modernity stretching back to the Industrial Revolution – has forced the parish church to reconsider its own sense of place. It is not that long ago that parish churches were the only places within a community that could house debates, discussions and social gatherings. But their monopoly has been broken by the endemic pluralization of public space: taverns, cinemas, community halls, as well as competing denominations and a host of other arenas. Arguably, the media, as the purveyor of information, recording and memory is the new public space. It would appear then, that parish churches are beginning to lose their point.

But it would be premature to sound the death knell for the parish church. My narration of the Parish Church in English cultural history clearly suggests that its identity has always been evolving, so there is arguably little cause for alarm. Every generation of churchwardens has had to face an apparently insuperable set of problems ranging from apathy to poverty through to clerical negligence and absence. All that we may say here is that the parish church is losing its identity because the concept and feel of parish-type communities has been lost first. The next line of defence, then, is for the recognition of *local* churches, and that is arguably the key mutation of modernity for the parish church: its identity is shifting from the parochial to the local – as the church that people know and identify with as their own.

Perhaps the churches need to panic a little less about the apparently bleak statistics, and their apparent loss of identity, and concentrate a little more on maintaining religion as something that is public, accessible and extensive, whilst also being distinct, intensive, and mysterious. I have five general comments to make by way of conclusion.

1. Even in the most modern societies, there is still demand for religion that is public, performative and pastoral. Many churches have seen a rise in numbers since September 11. Religion mutates and lives on; to take advantage of this, churches must continue to try to be open to the world and extensively engaged with their communities. Churches are often the only bodies within a community that provide public and open places for tears, grief, remembrance, laughter and celebration.

2. Religion is remarkably resilient in the modern age. Much of our 'vernacular religion' – such as the celebration of Christmas – reveals a nation that still enjoys its carols, nativity plays and other Christian artefacts that long ago moved beyond the control of the church to become part of the cultural furniture. Religion is still in demand. And here, parish churches have particular responsibilities to connect with vernacular religion, nascent spirituality and local cultures that show some yearning for the transcendent.

3. The churches can respond to the challenge of an apparently faithless age with a confidence founded on society (yes, society), which refuses to leave religion alone. Often the best that churches can do is to recover their poise within their social and cultural situations, and continue to offer a ministry and a faith to a public that wishes to relate to religion, without necessarily belonging to it.

4. The future of the parish church cannot be disconnected from its ecumenical context. Increasingly, parish churches have to come to terms with the different and similar ministries offered by other Christian communities within the same area. Granted, competition can be the engine of increase. But increasingly, collaboration, and actively working to preserve a dynamic mixed economy of ministry, looks like a worth while missiological strategy. Parish churches, rather than stretching themselves to the limit in all things, may be able to contemplate a degree of specialization within a culture of collaboration.

5. Although the accent of this chapter has been very much centred on places, there can be no question that the more contested, fluid and ambiguous spatial identity becomes, the more vital it is to make sure that ministries engage with people. This may mean congregations and parishes taking a more adventurous (and risky?) look at the intentional building of faith communities within particular niches. This may involve fresh expressions of chaplaincy (for example, in the workplace), or new ways of being church that may not have an obvious spatial rootedness. The Church, after all, is constantly seeking after the lost, the dislocated and those who have no place – those who feel no tie or loyalty to their

immediate environment. There must be a church for them too – further expression of Jesus' love.

So the recipe for the idea of the parish church might look like this: cultivate a relaxed awareness of the opportunities that surround us all; have faith in the resilience of God and the church; but also respond to the many tests of faith that dominate every age with tenacity, compassion and wisdom. Be confident in the buildings too; they are 'signs' of God's presence in the community. A tatty church suggests a neglected God. A neat, modern, comfortable (but otherwise invisible building) might suggest a private God. But a beautifully kept building, fit for few other purposes other than worship, suggests, funnily enough, life and otherness – something in the world, yet not of it. The parish church and the Christian faith have many more supporters than members. We do not live in a secular age: our era continues to be a time of questions, exploration, wonder and awe. The offering of an open building, and an outward-looking worshipping community, remain dominant signs on the cultural landscape, pointing to nothing less than the deep generosity and openness of God, who promises his people that 'there are many rooms in my Father's house'.

The gradual atrophy in the pivotal power of the English parish church since the Industrial Revolution is, in one sense, undeniable. At the same time, a detailed history of parish churches shows that their success and failure, prior to the Industrial Revolution, is not linked to secularization, and that spirituality and vernacular religion persist, waxing and waning, with or without due regard to the provision of parochial places of worship. Having said that, with parish churches no longer linked to the *local* economy and what that space generates in terms of wealth and income, those churches may have to re-invent themselves as places of worship, offering both intensive and extensive connectedness.

The parish church has always been a complex pottage of competing convictions and interests, brought together in the focus of a building and a ministry, the ownership of which has always been open to interpretation. What the parish church needs now, arguably, is to continually rediscover its ministry, one that engages with culture in creative ways. The shift from the *parochial* to the *local* might not be entirely deleterious. In the future, patterns of ministry will no longer be configured solely through geographical space and its constraints. For the Church to find its place in the modern world, it will have to create new spaces for new communities and different opportunities for differentiated niche groups. Such a vision might appear to threaten the very concept of a parish church; but it might also be its saviour. To be a parish church, a church must find a community and locate itself within it, incarnating the life of God there in ways that are both local and catholic. In the complex, porous and ambiguous spaces of our future, the Church will need to find its places in society once again, if it is to continue to offer a religion that is public, performative and pastoral.

2

On the analyst's couch: Psychological perspectives on congregations and clergy

Sara Savage

Sara Savage is a social psychologist and Senior Researcher with the Psychology and Religion Research Programme in the University of Cambridge. She writes here on the parish system viewed from a psychologist's perspective in this time of change. It is, she argues, a system characterized by generosity with many positives. However, particularly for the clergy, there is also a darker side, which needs to be admitted and faced and which can become a source of growth and healing.

When viewed from a psychologist's perspective, is the parish system more gift than burden? What are the taken-for-granted positives – and what are the negatives that shackle the unwary, ministers and congregations alike? Can these be transformed to foster a healthy social dynamic in the parish?

From my psychologist's chair, my chief impression is that the parish system is remarkably generous. This generosity is demonstrated through clergy and the committed core seeking to extend spiritual care to *all*. In Britain's post-Christian context, this inevitably takes an attenuated form. The open-handedness of the parish system reflects the grace of the gospel, yet, like an over-generous woman, now risks depletion. So the time is ripe to lay out the parish system, as it were, on the analyst's couch.

Each parish will present its own unique combination of luminous positives with exhausting negatives. But first, honour is due to the social-psychological benefits of the parish system. These will be discussed briefly before plunging into the focus of this chapter: the psychological processes that burden clergy and congregations.

A glance at the positives

The open-handed generosity of the parish system enables a sense of ownership and ease of access in a number of ways:

- The parish church, as a landmark and a sacred place, is 'owned' by attenders and non-attenders alike.
- The outreach potential through occasional services, schools, and links with wider society encourage ongoing evangelistic opportunities.
- Links with wider society minimize social-psychological distance between church and culture, thus easing access and conversion.
- Ideally suited to our privacy-loving society, parish church protocol is rarely invasive; introverts can remain intact if they so desire.
- The cognitive and emotional complexity fostered by the Church's rich heritage of art, music, architecture, and liturgy deepens religious knowing and nourishes ongoing faith development.
- The range of theological perspectives within Anglicanism speaks of a diverse, organic, supple community.
- Checks and balances in the system of church governance work to a fair degree. While not unknown, religious abuse is relatively rare.

Where else in society are these very British, luminous positives so generously lavished? Yet, as in all human systems, paradox and contradiction prevail. These positives possess an underside. Such is the generosity of the parish system that the burdensome costs of the positive features are borne mainly by the clergy, the focus of the next section.

The complex nature of the 'positives'

Sacred place

The psychology of sacred place is a powerful, if spiritually ambivalent, ally to the parish system. From pre-history, deeply ingrained in the human psyche is an attachment to a local sacred place, where a meeting between heaven and earth is understood to occur. The church building provides a physical symbol which structures a world view in which it is conceivable – even today – for God and humans to interact. People *belong* to the community and the space thus hallowed by the parish church.[1] Church buildings, visual reminders of the sacred canopy, thus foster a sense of belonging for the whole parish.

Yet, sacred buildings can also provide an opt-out clause, a 'vicarious' form of religion:[2] '*My* parish church (or *my* vicar) will do my religion for me'. This loyalty is restricted: few rural congregations are interested in wider team services; their psychological investment is in their local parish church. The forced closure of a village church beloved by a tiny, ageing congregation shuts down a deep impulse towards genuine community. This impulse is not easily re-ignited by the 'option' of attending a town centre church somewhere else. So, the faithful few struggle to keep rural churches open while the over-stretched clergy are compelled to fund-raise for church repairs from an ever-shrinking pool.

It appears that the psychology of sacred place pertains most strongly in rural or small town parishes. For 'gathered' churches, usually in suburban or urban settings the loyalty of church attenders is often not to the parish church per se, but to a 'stream' of Christianity of which the parish church is seen as a good example. These streams have particular ways of 'doing' Christianity, each with their own summer camps, festivals, books, speakers, magazines, web sites. They may be evangelical, post evangelical, charismatic, liberal, Anglo-catholic or any combination of these. If another church nearby (perhaps of a different denomination) is seen as a better exemplar of the 'stream', then church hopping readily occurs. The networked, mobile nature of streams nests quite comfortably within the parish system (and probably benefits from it), but here the commitment of *members* does not feed into the parish system per se, but rather to the stream.

A number of 'gathered' churches are large and thriving, enjoying gifted laity eager to be involved in a range of lay ministries. However, these gifted members also demand much from their church involvement and, as consumers, will go elsewhere if their desire for a transformed personal life and a caring community go unmet. The clergy have much to attain, juggling their duties as parish priest with civic and pastoral responsibilities as well. Some do this extremely well. For others, the range of skills required by high-profile gathered churches is daunting.

Woven into the fabric of life

Church schools,[3] parish-wide occasional services, hospital, prison, and industrial chaplaincies, along with an ever-growing range of community-based church endeavours provide multiple links between the church and wider society. Yet here too, this positive feature casts a shadow. While conversion or entry into the church is made easier through minimizing social distance from the 'host' culture, this occurs at the cost of parish churches having fuzzy boundaries.

Fuzzy boundaries fall short of making clear 'us' and 'them' distinctions. Churches that demand much of members result in a clear in-group contrasted with a derogated out-group. This contrast seems to foster religious commitment, despite, or perhaps due to, a lack of charity towards outsiders! Marketing experts have noticed a similar trend: 'Unless this perfume is really expensive, it's not worth buying.' The motive to maintain positive self-esteem by belonging to a clearly defined 'elite' group is pervasive: 'Why should I attend church X unless it is the best, the most true, the most blessed?'

In contrast, parish churches allow for a gradual growing into the faith. There is no embarrassing fanfare to be endured. Most of us do not remember our baptisms; we simply 'belong'. It is possible to belong to a parish church, experience support and spiritual nourishment without undue social invasion. It is also possible to drift away, unremarked. For a country of introverts (or so the cultural myth proclaims), the parish system provides an unthreatening entree into the Christian faith. The privacy thus secured is often highly valued and fiercely protected. This sometimes (secretly) takes the form of 'we would rather let the church die than change'.

Churches and conformity

Like all social groups, churches encourage conformity to group norms, whether reverent genuflection or exuberant speaking in tongues. In the case of parish churches, group norms usually echo, and are strengthened by, traditional British cultural norms: be polite, be moderate, keep a stiff upper lip, don't be an exhibitionist. For example, contrast the spiritual reality generated *during* a communion service, with the moment the faithful are dismissed for coffee. In an instant, the profound sense of shared spirituality vanishes as social norms and polite, mundane conversation take over. Dissenters who might challenge such group norms appear odd, and are usually 'frozen' out.

People coming into parish churches sense these unwritten rules, and find it an uphill slog to introduce changes (even spiritually enriching changes). The more innovative or religiously intense parishioners often give up and go elsewhere. Within the soft embrace of an acquiescing majority, a great deal of social loafing can occur. Bums on pews are often just that. It falls to the clergy to motivate this settled blancmange.

The argument here is that *parish* church norms are under-girded by *wider* cultural norms, thus intensifying the usual drift towards conformity in churches. And so the power of conformity seems unassailable. In contrast, the influence of a minority is in fact a more potent and innovative force.[4] Even a small minority has the power to challenge taken-for-granted norms and to bring about a conversion of attitudes, but only under these conditions:

- unity
- showing consistency over time
- with a clearly expressed message.

Parish church attenders are few in number, but miss out on wielding their *potential* minority influence in our post Christian culture. Of the three factors that empower a minority, the extroversion required to express a message clearly seems furthest from reach.

Cultural richness and complexity

Perhaps the greatest strength of the parish system comes through its inheritance of sacred art, music, architecture, liturgy, scholarship and range of theological perspectives. Combined with the rhythm of the Church year, and well-educated clergy, these factors richly nourish Christian education and formation. In a deprived, urban context this richness can be psychologically empowering: 'this beauty is your spiritual home.' The liturgy enables services to proceed with relatively little dependence upon the personality of the presiding minister (which may indeed be a blessing!). Subtle or unintended manipulation of a congregation's emotions is thereby lessened; a private inner space for 'deep' processing of input and quiet prayer is preserved.

The range of stimuli in, for example, a parish Eucharist, involves all the senses through word, movement, taste, music, symbol, and silence. Religious knowing (how people acquire knowledge of the things of God) is a complex endeavour; it is not so much about coming to know a separate 'religious world', as coming to know the religious dimension of the entire everyday world.[5] It is a knowing that must involve us emotionally and experientially, as well as intellectually. It must transform us as well as transform our perceptions of the world.

The down side is that this rich heritage is foreign territory for the unchurched mass. Clergy spend so much energy getting people *into* church and making services accessible that a certain dumbing down is inevitable. In many parishes, there is little time or energy left over to equip more mature Christians for the onward journey – where the Church's rich and complex heritage would come into its own. Churches which have the person power able to offer a range of specialist services (youth services, seeker services, 'godly play' for children, meditative Eucharist, alternative worship, men's breakfast, Taizé services, and so forth) have a better chance of connecting with a greater range of people at different stages of faith development, age, or interest groups. Thus, a polarizing of churches into the 'haves' and 'have nots' is emerging across the parish system.

Checks and balances

Around 20 years ago people were leaving the Church of England in droves to join independent, and/or charismatic house churches. A number are now drifting back to parish churches, looking for a less authoritarian approach. Checks and balances provided by the system of church governance make most parish churches psychologically 'safe' places where religious abuse (an abuse of religious power) is rare.

Painful lessons have been learned following a small number of well-documented situations where things went badly wrong. The Church's now heightened awareness of the possibility of religious abuse (including child abuse) strengthens the normal checks and balances provided by PCCs, church wardens, synods, and the higher levels of church leadership.

This vigilance is positive and necessary, but, alas, it is also possible that the checks and balances can work too well, preventing clergy from initiating needed change. Members who have been pillars of the church for decades have a sense of ownership, and an implicit power base, which may survive an incumbency of a mere five, seven or ten years. A very dominant church warden can make it difficult for a PCC to vote in a new warden, despite the new six-year ruling. While a system of checks and balances is imperative, a cocktail of dominant or difficult personalities in influential positions can shackle an incumbent. Clergy can feel powerless in the face of internal 'cabals'.

Summary of the positives

To summarize so far, the positive features of the parish system (the power of sacred place, the Church's normative position in society easing entry into the Christian faith, the abundant artistic, liturgical and theological heritage, the checks and balances of parish church governance) are valuable indeed. Yet the generous nature of the parish system goes largely unsung: few parishioners realize that the heavy costs of maintaining the positives are borne mainly by the clergy.

The 'negative' features of the parish system

We now turn to the main focus for this chapter and examine the psychologically dark side of church life. These features are termed 'negative' simply because the shadows are cast more widely: they touch not only clergy but committed members as well. Fringe attenders and newcomers are often blissfully unaware that a dark side attends the genuinely warm welcome they have received. (They will become disillusioned when they do!). The ray of hope here is that the negative features of church life are its *growth point*; change and healing in these dimensions, while difficult, produce a radiant authenticity in church life. I will be highlighting some practical resources and strategic responses to the challenges thrown up by this section.

Hierarchy

Church buildings describe a hierarchically arranged universe in which the laity take up their allotted place. Not disputing the fact that all organizations need leadership, contemporary culture sits oddly with this hierarchical system, with its echoes of feudal society. People quickly intuit who has power in any given group, and modify their behaviour accordingly. Hierarchies are known to elicit certain behaviours, for example: status seeking, fawning, bullying, passivity, blaming others, fearing criticism, and gossiping (the currency of the disempowered).[6] Basically, people try to 'work' a hierarchy to their own advantage, lest they become oppressed by it. As seen in nature, hierarchies are stable, but they are not liberating. Many churches hope that their small groups (such as home groups) will mitigate the formality of hierarchy, and to some extent they do. But then people swing back to hierarchical behaviours on Sundays or at PCCs.

In the west, people no longer live their lives according to fixed roles.[7] Our culture is one of mobile portfolio careers, combined families, fluid relationships seeking intimacy,[8] re-invented identities. In earlier eras, it was sufficient to fulfil one's given social role. In that earlier social context, church life based on hierarchically attuned behaviour was appropriate, even necessary. Now it seems a backward step. No longer does it provide the social modelling which will equip people to live Christian lives in the contemporary context. Hierarchy, however benign, as a way of 'doing relationships', is, for many, a thing of the past.

The norm of niceness

Clergy are *expected* to be nice. This softens the impact of hierarchy, while preserving it. The norm of Christian niceness is ubiquitous, despite the portrait the Gospels paint of Jesus as an assertive, sometimes acerbic personality who readily confronted people in order to pursue their spiritual welfare.

The demographics of parish church attenders interact with the norm of niceness. The industrialized West has seen a decline of face-to-face community. In many parishes, the people who are available for local community gatherings (of any sort) are the retired or women with young or growing children. Teenagers have their own friendship networks outside the church via communication technologies and immersion in the popular arts,[9] and much of the working adult population are busy commuting. Those who do show up on a Sunday morning bring a certain flavour, which, for the sake of the children, could be described as 'nice' or even anodyne.

While nastiness is clearly unproductive, the norm of niceness can tie churches up in knots. This is, of course, in the context of church life heavily reliant on the good will of volunteers and many in official but unpaid roles. Volunteer workers for example, are, in general, relatively intolerant of conflict in comparison to paid employees (who realize they simply have to put up with it). Volunteer workers expect appreciation and a good deal of freedom to carry out their activities in their own way. They do not expect to be confronted by the 'nice' vicar over a procedural disagreement.

Given the human tendency to 'want things our own way', examining the motives for ministry should pertain as much to volunteer lay involvement as it does to clergy, who at least are screened by trained selectors. Yet, by necessity it is believed, volunteers are taken on trust. In so doing, churches offer 'small fish' an opportunity to be 'big fish'. Churches offer people an opportunity to defend their world view. Volunteer workers (as well as clergy) sometimes take their stand 'on principle', a verbal signal that genuine discussion is now disbarred. Voices are raised in a tell-tale way. World views are at stake. Power is at stake. How best to express leadership in this emotion-laden context is a mystery for many. This kind of problem arises less often in secular organizations as these have the freedom to be hard-hearted and weed out the 'wrong' people. The generous, trusting (naïve?) tendency in parishes may go a long way to explain why churches are so often less effective as organizations than their secular counterparts.

Conflict

An uneven relationship thus ensues between clergy and volunteers. Clergy desperately need their lay workers and volunteers, of whom there is a limited supply. (Organists know this.) A collaborative approach is desirable, but these relationships can easily swing from the minister being too directive, thus spoiling it for the volunteer, to the minister having too little authority, even being bullied. There exists a well-known conflict between those who are more mission minded (often the clergy) and those who are more maintenance minded.[10] Similar problems exist in ministry teams, yet few are practised in the skills needed for resolving conflicts face to face. Indeed, a high proportion of vicar–curate relationships are reported to be unsatisfactory. None of these tensions is helped by the pervasive norm to be polite and to 'not upset anyone'.

Without the skills to resolve conflicts directly, indirect hostility is an easy way for congregations to control their clergy. Gossip is usually the weapon of choice. In response, the pulpit can offer clergy a safe place from which to tell people off. It is obvious that in organizations as complex as churches, conflict is unavoidable. Yet to tackle conflict one has to surmount a taboo: the belief that church should be a conflict-free zone of heavenly peace. Far from being a sign of failure, conflict is a growth point; it is a rare arena in which religious people are forced to relate honestly to one another. Collaborative win/win solutions take a great deal of maturity and skill to achieve. Compromise, where both parties win some and lose some, are perhaps a little easier to achieve. These two conflict resolution styles are riskier, more exposing, but often more productive.[11] It can be easier simply to compete and impose one's own dictates, if feeling strong, or to acquiesce, if feeling weak. Avoidance is perhaps the most prevalent of the five styles of conflict resolution in 'nice' churches. An acidic tone of voice can alone swing the vote of a PCC meeting, as everyone present, peace-loving Christians one and all, seek to avoid an impending conflict.

All five conflict resolution styles are appropriate in church if used with transparency and a commitment to be constructive. Relationships are more secure once they have negotiated conflict. Being realistic, most church leaders need outside support and training to equip them to resolve conflicts effectively. Clearly, conflict resolution needs to be taught throughout ministerial and post-ministerial training. The London Mennonite Centre has made conflict resolution in churches a cornerstone of its ministry of peacemaking. Scores of clergy and church workers, ground down by bitter disputes, or even on the brink of a church split, have benefited from the Centre's skilled mediation, or from the practical and sensitively run training courses in handling conflict in churches. (A brief list of materials and resources can be found at the end of the chapter.)

Difficult people

I am reliably informed that one of the most stressful features of ministry is the effort to be nice to 'difficult people'. Defining others as difficult can be, of course, a projection of one's own personality problems. However, it is salutary to realize that according to the Diagnostic Statistical Manual IV (the manual that categorizes the range of psychological disorders), there is a small portion of the population, who, while not psychotic (in other words, they are in touch with reality) have developed inflexible, maladaptive personalities with a striking inability to reflect on their own need for change. Thus the clinical outlook for those afflicted is bleak.

People suffering from personality disorders often avoid social groups such as church. Yet people with a *narcissistic* personality disorder can in fact be attracted to the way a religious belief system provides a pretext for self-righteousness and self-centredness. Narcissists are marked by an inability to see another's point of view.[12] They can be charming and outwardly successful, but other people are not 'real' for narcissists; they are objects that should conform to the narcissist's 'correct' point of view. Ministerial selection processes usually manage to screen clergy in this regard, but no similar mechanism exists for screening lay volunteers. Given this lack of screening, at times the wrong people will get into influential positions in church. Personality disorders are a matter of degree, and the categories are much contested among psychologists. Suffice it to say, even a slight degree of narcissistic personality disorder in the context of a 'nice' church will create inordinate distress. This is especially the case if the difficult person also has a position of social power within the parish.

Theological training rarely includes 'handling difficult people' on the syllabus (although it should!). Handling difficult people requires compassion and firm boundaries, as in one vicar's pithy advice: 'Form a real relationship with them, and then sit on them.'

Variety and disunity

Many of us are drawn to the Church of England because it is a broad church acknowledging the validity of different approaches. How liberating; how refreshing! Alas, very soon we find ourselves participating in the mutual hostility and misapprehension that marks interactions between those of different theological orientations. Diocesan email networks exhibit 'flaming'; bitter arguments erupt at synods of all levels between clergy of different traditions, even over the most mundane issues. Leaders, at all levels in the hierarchy, may seek to advance their own theological orientation in such a way as to disadvantage others. Clergy intuit this, and feel they have to fight their corner, an issue not unrelated to preferment (or a decent job).

Theological and moral disputes are complicated by organizational structure. Given the nature of church, without an agreed 'Alpha male' to impose order, factions 'wage war'. On the diocesan level, it is not always clear who has the upper hand. At present, there is an odd disjunction between status and power. Those who have status (for example, bishops) do not necessarily have the power to resolve situations, especially with clergy who hold the freehold of their livings. Those who do not have status (but may desire it) might enjoy throwing their weight around. This open field may be a good thing in principle, but well-developed conflict resolution skills are required to bring about mature outcomes. One solution at least is straightforward: on-going training in conflict resolution needs to become a regular feature of ministerial training.

Unconscious processes

The plot thickens. The Christian life involves movement towards wholeness of personality, and this involves a re-working of unhealthy relationships which defined us as we grew up. Discipleship involves re-parenting. It is inevitable, therefore, that in church life various unconscious forces are passed back and forth between clergy and congregation. Research by Rizutto[13] and others discuss the complex manner in which, from infancy onwards, the psyche's unconscious God image develops as a result of interactions and relationships with mother, father, and carers. The God image then acts as a 'lens' through which people view God. It is normal that God's 'representatives', the clergy, evoke strong feelings, and that emotions from significant past relationships are transferred on to them. This process of transference may be signalled by inordinate love towards the minister, or, if failing to comply with a person's particular God image, inordinate hate.

Balanced teaching about the nature of God is necessary – but not sufficient – to help transform how people relate at a deep level to God and to others. It is through the messiness of real relationships within church that people grapple with, and transform, their less-than-accurate God image. When a minister senses that he or she has become embroiled in transference, help from a spiritual director or trained counsellor is a sensible first step.

The pressure for clergy to maintain an excessively nice pulpit persona may result in 'irritable clergy syndrome' at home or among other clergy. Clergy may be lambs led to the slaughter in the context of their own congregations, but at deanery and diocesan level they can be dragons defending 'the truth'.

Under such a load, it is very difficult for clergy to form normal relationships within the church. This sets a negative model, and discourages real relationships from developing among church members. Everyone has to be on good behaviour. This erosion of the freedom to be an authentic self undermines the springs of spiritual and psychological well-being. A religious performance is then substituted, particularly if less-than-conscious erroneous beliefs are operating among clergy:[14]

1. I must be successful in everything I do.

2. Everyone must accept me.

3. Everyone must love me.

4. If I make a mistake I am a total failure.

5. If I disagree with someone they won't like me.

6. My value as a person depends on how other people view me.

Holding these kinds of beliefs, clergy are likely to feel swamped by people's expectations. How can a minister break through this impasse? It clearly would not be helpful for ministers to over-expose their own sins and weaknesses. Maintaining personal boundaries balanced with a degree of honest self-disclosure is at the heart of healthy relationships. How can this become normative in the church? One approach comes from the Beta course,[15] a pastoral care course designed to help people re-learn how to do healthy relationships in the context of church life. Beta is a safe process enabling personal transformation, establishing boundaries of confidentiality and privacy, without missing out on the liberation of sharing with fellow Christians the challenges of our human experience.

Risks in pastoral ministry

Ministers are called upon to enter into people's lives at times of great vulnerability. In secular practice, people who counsel others are normally required to have in-depth counselling and ongoing supervision. There is no corollary for this in pastoral ministry.

A large-scale piece of research in the USA by Blackmon[16] revealed that 37 per cent of clergy admitted to involvement in sexual behaviour inappropriate to the ministry role (either inside or outside the congregation, or both). This ranges from sexual overtures, to harassment, to abuse. This is three to four times higher than in other caring professions that have intimate dealing with clients. Why is this? It certainly is not because ministers have lower moral standards for themselves or others.

Why does it happen? Clergy are in what is termed by Malony and Hunt as 'dual role relationships'[17] with their parishioners; they are in more than one role with client. The clergy person can become immensely significant to the counsellee. This can lead to grandiosity on the part of the minister, resulting in poor judgement, the blurring of boundaries and misreading emotional vulnerability as a sexual invitation. This is all the more likely to happen if the clergy 'need to be needed'. Most dioceses provide confidential clergy / family counselling for such times of crisis. Prevention is needed too. The skills of maintaining healthy relationship boundaries drawing on the insights of counselling psychology need to be taught as a normal part of ministerial formation.

Clergy may feel they need to be 'God' to their flock. Yet, surprisingly, attempting to meet all pastoral needs (an impossible task) is not even what most people are looking for, according to Francis and Richter's research into why people leave churches.[18] A factor of *least* importance for church leavers was the lack of professionalized clergy pastoral care. What people were often looking for, and not finding, is church as a caring community.

Clergy stress

Now sprinkle in to these problematic church dynamics the unique occupational pressures of ministry. A toxic cocktail can result. John Davey[19] points out factors to do with the nature of the job of ministry itself:

- *Role conflict:* A minister may feel called to a priestly role and instead finds that he or she is needed as an administrator and manager of ancient church property.
- *Role overload:* Clergy are rarely fully off duty. Emergency pastoral calls can come at any time. There are no fixed hours; the task is never done. The shortfall between seemingly infinite demands (eight rural parishes) and resources (one vicar) are intensified by feelings of powerlessness when faced with others' intense suffering at times of tragedy, or in urban priority areas marked by unemployment, poverty or racism.
- *Role ambiguity:* A congregation and minister may have very different

implicit ideas of the role of the minister, but these are rarely articulated. The goals of ministry are fuzzy (for example, bringing in the kingdom of God). How does a minister measure success in this realm?

Clergy stress cannot be solved simply by heroic actions on the part of the stressed individual. Usually some sort of organizational change is needed at the local church as well. Church consultancy can help in this regard, for example, by enabling divergent expectations of the role of the minister and congregation to be explored in a safe, constructive manner. Through wise facilitation on the part of the church consultant, the church can discover its own solutions to problems that previously felt too overwhelming, or deeply rooted, to tackle. Church consultancy gently reveals how things really are in a church. From that growth point, the consultant supports the clergy and church representatives to find their own solutions, rather than imposing an idealized version about how church should be.[20] The outcome is growth in maturity and openness, as all participants in the consultancy process take responsibility for how things are, and how they would like things to be. (Organizations offering different kinds of church consultancy can be found at the end of this chapter.)

The stressors for clergy are enormous, but so too is the satisfaction of following their call. Many clergy report that they wouldn't to want to do anything else. This sincere commitment can unfortunately entwine with a tendency to deny personal difficulties. The psychological skills and resources are now available to help ministers steer the negative dimensions of parish life into more wholesome directions. The argument here is that these resources need to become a normal part of ordination and post-ordination training. Clergy who maintain a confidential support network of friends and family, have an array of ongoing input (mentoring, spiritual direction, counselling, church consultancy), learn the social skills of team management, empowering leadership, conflict resolution and assertiveness, refresh themselves through education, retreats and sabbaticals, and engage in a variety of forms of ministry and community-based projects, may be hardier in the face of occupational stress. If the worst does happen, there are a number of excellent ministries to help burned-out ministers regain their well-being (see end of chapter). Of course, prevention is better than cure.

A final note: This chapter has been written with stipendiary ministry as the assumed norm. Non-stipendiary ministers (NSMs) (and (lay) Readers) often juggle a full-time career alongside their ministry, comprising a courageous workload. This may force NSMs from the outset to be more selective in what they do. They may be targets of fewer projections and unrealistic expectations than stipendiary clergy, and thus able to work in a less trammelled way. Conversely, they may feel they have less influence and status, but is this a drawback for servant leadership? Indeed, some of the structural changes forced on the Church by shrinking finances already promote lay and non-stipendiary ministry.

Conclusion

Every church will have different ratios of positive and negative features. Consequently, there is no one-size-fits-all solution. And something else is afoot – the reality of faith. A final irony is that the overwhelming generosity of God's blessing and presence among Christians (interpreted as a deserved reward?) may delay our recognition that anything is amiss with religious organizations!

The frailty of the over-generous parish system is all too evident, yet this vulnerability can also be seen as a mark of journeying with Christ. Given the rate of cultural change during the latter part of this journey, it is clear that a host of 'fresh expressions' of church is needed if the church is to re-connect with culture. However, it is not possible to shed the problems discussed in this chapter simply by starting new forms of church. Embedded in the human condition as the 'negatives' are, the dark side of church will persist in fresh expressions, although this will not be evident until the honeymoon period is over. We need to guard against fantasy solutions that make us think we can leave the current problems behind simply by creating new forms of church (though this will be difficult enough!). We need to learn from the social psychological processes endemic in the parish system. These normal, social processes need to be tackled in their own right, drawing on the resources mentioned in this chapter, so that they become a normal part of ministerial formation and church life.

In summary, I have argued that the generous positives of church life possess an underside, the cost of which is borne largely by the clergy. Further, the positives, in the face of church decline, are attended by a fear of loss which results in constricted thinking. The harder people cling to the positives, the more exhausting are the conflicts produced by the negatives. Yet, these negative features, while daunting, contain a germ of hope.

As a psychologist, I am sorely tempted to give advice. If the parish system could be condensed into a single 'patient on the couch', my advice would be:

Stop clinging to the positives. Let them float on the water. What can survive, will survive. Face into the negatives. Develop the means to deal with them; use the resources that exist. Trust the process of change. Change is necessary and will occur whether it is welcomed or not. To welcome change is to trust that the Church always has been, and will continue to be, a wise householder bringing out treasures both old and new.

Resources

Clergy stress
The Claybury Trust
The Pixmore Centre
Pixmore Avenue
Letchworth Garden City
Herts
SG6 1JG
www.claybury.org

The Society of Mary and Martha
Dunsford
Exeter
EX6 7LE
www.sheldon.uk.com

Pastoral care, healthy church dynamics
The Beta Course
Faculty of Divinity
University of Cambridge
West Road
Cambridge
CB3 9BS
www.beta-course.org

Conflict resolution and mediation
The London Mennonite Centre
14 Shepherds Hill
Highgate
London
N6 5AQ
www.menno.org.uk

Leadership, church consultancy
The Grubb Institute
Cloudesley Street
London
N1 0HU
www.grubb.org.uk

The Leadership Institute
Tel. 01227–479706
www.tli.org.uk

Arrow Leadership Training, CPAS
Foundation for Church Leadership
4 Portal Road
York
YO26
www.churchleadershipfoundation.org

Further reading

F. Watts, R. Nye and S. Savage, *Psychology for Christian Ministry*, Routledge, 2002, particularly the following chapters:
Clergy
Social processes
The church as an organization
Unhealthy religion
Diversity among Christians
The psychology of church services

3

From obligation to consumption: Understanding the patterns of religion in Northern Europe

Grace Davie

Grace Davie is Professor of the Sociology of Religion at the University of Exeter and is a leading thinker in her field. She offers an introduction to three key concepts, all of which concern the evolving relationship between church and society: believing without belonging, vicarious religion and a shift from a religion of obligation to one characterized by choice. This primarily sociological analysis has been constructed to provide an overview of current trends in both belief and practice from a Northern European perspective. Grace concludes by offering some general guidelines to those responsible for charting a pathway for churches in Britain in the twenty-first century.

Believing without belonging[1]

What is happening to religious life in Northern Europe? From a sociological perspective there is a mismatch between different measurements and disagreement about what they mean.[2]

On the one hand we have a set of indicators that measure firm commitments to institutional life and credal statements of religion (in this case Christianity). All of these display a marked reduction in Europe as a whole, but most of all in the Protestant nations in the North – hence the reputation of countries such as Britain or Sweden as some of the most secular in the world.[3]

These indicators are, of course, closely related to each other in so far as institutional commitment (in the form of religious membership or regular practice) both reflects and confirms religious belief *in its orthodox forms*. The believing Christian attends church to express his or her belief and to receive affirmation that this is the right thing to do. At the same time, repeated exposure to the institution and its teaching necessarily informs, not to say disciplines, belief.

No observer of the current religious scene disputes these facts – that is, that these dimensions of European religion are both interrelated and in serious decline. There is, on the other hand, considerable debate about the consequences of this situation. The complex relationship between belief (in a *wider* sense) and practice is central to this discussion, for it is clear that a manifest reduction in the 'hard' indicators of religious life has not, *in the short term at least*, had a similar effect on rather less rigorous dimensions of religiousness. Indeed, the resultant mismatch in the different indicators is the principal finding of the various enquiries carried out under the auspices of the European Values Study;[4] it is supported by almost all empirical investigations of the current religious scene in Northern Europe. It is precisely this state of affairs that was captured by the phrase 'believing without belonging'.

What happened next was unexpected (not least to me): despite the fact that as an idea 'believing without belonging' was hardly new, 'the expression has rapidly spread across the world and beyond the borders of scholarship'.[5] More precisely, the phrase has become a reference point for a wide variety of audiences, both in the academy and outside it. Some idea of the extent of this discussion can be found by putting 'believing without belonging' into an Internet search engine. The phrase appears everywhere: in academic papers all over the world, in more popular writing about the churches in this country and in others, in the statements of religious leaders (and indeed of followers), in religious journalism, and (not least) in A-level exam papers. Quite clearly, the notion resonates for many, very different, groups of people. Voas and Crockett provide a helpful categorization of this discussion into hard and soft versions of the 'theory', before embarking on a series of empirically based criticisms. These criticisms will not be dealt with here except where they coincide with the argument as a whole; they will be answered in full in the new edition of the 1994 book.[6] In this chapter, something rather different is required: a clarification of two or three key themes within the believing without belonging debate in order that the concept itself be properly understood.

The first clarification concerns the status or even the state of established churches of Northern Europe as, *de facto* if not *de jure*, one type of voluntary organization among many. If it is true that the churches as institutions have declined markedly in the post-war period, the same process (declines in membership, financial support and so on) can be seen in almost all social activities which require people to 'gather' on a regular basis (political parties, trade unions, team sports etc.). Situating the churches within this broader economic and social context is crucial if we are to understand what is happening. It immediately becomes clear, for example, that the reduction in church activity in Western Europe forms part of a profound change in the nature of social life; it is not, in contrast, an unequivocal indicator of religious indifference. It becomes, in fact, a central feature of the wider, and politically urgent, discussions of social capital that are taking place on both sides of the Atlantic.[7] Or to express the same idea rather more provocatively: believing without belonging is a pervasive dimension of modern European societies – it is not confined to the religious lives of European people.

A second point reflects the attitudes of church leaders. Understandably enough, significant numbers of individuals charged with the maintenance of Europe's religious organizations have fallen upon the phrase 'believing without belonging' in order to justify their continued existence – arguing that things are not as bad as they seem. As it happens, I do think that the churches have a continuing existence in Northern Europe, but for reasons that require careful and detailed consideration (see below). In the meantime, it is important that the churches' personnel appreciate that the situation described by this phrase is neither better nor worse than a more straightforwardly (if one may use that term) secular society. It is simply different. Those that minister to a half-believing rather than unbelieving society will find that there are advantages and disadvantages to this situation, as there are in any other. Working out appropriate ministerial strategies for this continually shifting and ill-defined context is the central and very demanding task of the religious professional. A firm and necessary grasp of the sociological realities is only the starting point.

A third question follows from this and relates to the remark concerning the short and long term. It is at this point, moreover, that the sociological debate intensifies. They are those (notably Bryan Wilson, Steve Bruce, Robin Gill and to some extent David Voas and Alasdair Crockett) who argue cogently that the mismatch between believing and belonging may well exist, but it is simply a temporary phenomenon; it is only a matter of time before belief – unsustained by regular attendance (that is, by an institution) – diminishes to match the more rigorous indicators of religiousness. In so far as this debate refers to statements of credal religion endorsed by the churches, I would agree with them. I am much less sure, however, about the looser and more heterodox elements of belief. Indeed, there are persuasive data emerging from the most recent enquiries of the European Values Study,[8] which indicate that the relationship between certain dimensions of belief and belonging may well be inverse rather than direct. Notable here are those aspects of belief which relate to the soul and to life after death.[9] These appear to rise markedly in *younger* rather than older generations, and in precisely those countries of Europe (mostly but not exclusively in the North) where the institutional capacities of the churches are most diminished.

With this in mind, the future becomes difficult to predict. What seems unlikely, however, is the emergence of a society in which secular rationalism becomes the overriding norm. It is more likely that looser forms of belief will go on existing alongside more secular understandings of life. The relationship between them will be long term and complex, rather than one simply replacing the other. Indeed a useful focus of research might lie in elucidating the particular circumstances in which one aspect of human living may predominate over the other. In other words, are there circumstances (both individual and collective) where the religious emerges as more rather than less significant and what forms of religion might be helpful in such circumstances? It is at this point that the discussion needs to take into account the connections between emergent patterns of belief and the institutional churches themselves, for it is clear that the latter continue not only to exist but to exert an influence on many aspects of individual and collective lives – even in Northern Europe.

Vicarious religion

The separating out of belief (with the emphasis on the individual) from belonging (giving due weight to the institution) has undoubtedly offered fruitful ways in which to understand and to organize the material about religion in modern Europe. Ongoing reflection about the current situation has, however, prompted me to reflect more deeply about the relationship between the two, utilizing, amongst other ideas, the notion of 'vicarious religion'.[10] By vicarious, I mean the notion of religion performed by an active minority but on behalf of a much larger number, *who (implicitly at least) not only understand, but quite clearly approve of what the minority is doing.*

More precisely, religion can operate vicariously in a variety of ways:[11]

● Churches and church leaders perform ritual on behalf of others (for example, at the time of a birth, a marriage, a divorce even, and above all at the time of a death). European populations are offended if these 'services' are denied.

36

- Church leaders and churchgoers believe on behalf of others. It is quite clear, for example, that church leaders should not doubt in public and get into trouble if they do.

- Church leaders and churchgoers embody moral codes on behalf of others. Religious professionals are expected to maintain moral standards in their private as well as public lives – a situation that imposes heavy burdens on the families of those in ministry.

- Rather more provocatively, churches can offer space for the vicarious debate of unresolved issues in modern societies. The current debate about homosexuality in the Anglican Communion offers a good example. Without such an explanation, it would be much harder to discover why the secular press pays such close attention to the discussion about senior appointments in a supposedly marginal institution.

My thinking about vicarious religion has been prompted very largely by the situation in the Nordic countries. A number of Nordic scholars have responded to the notion of believing without belonging by reversing the formula: the characteristic Nordic stance in terms of religion is to belong without believing.[12] Such scholars are entirely right in these observations. Nordic populations, for the most part, remain members of their Lutheran churches; they use them extensively for the occasional offices and regard membership as part of national just as much as religious identity. More pertinently for the churches themselves, Nordic people continue to pay appreciable amounts of tax to their churches – resulting, among other things, in large numbers of religious professionals (not least musicians) and beautifully maintained buildings in even the tiniest village. The cultural aspects of religion are well cared for.

This does not mean, of course, that Nordic populations attend their churches with any frequency, nor do they necessarily believe in the tenets of Lutheranism. Indeed, they appear on every comparative scale to be among the least believing and least practising populations in the world. So how should we understand their continuing membership of and support for their churches? This question is not only central to the understanding of religion in large parts of Europe, but poses a significant methodological challenge. How is it possible to get beneath the surface of the Nordic, or indeed any other, society in order to investigate the deep but largely hidden reflexes of a population? A second point follows from this: how do these reflexes not only connect with, but sustain the institutional churches, so often described as moribund in Northern Europe?

An iceberg may provide a helpful analogy. It is easy enough both to measure and to take note of the part that emerges from the water. Large numbers of studies have done precisely that and concluded that the visible tip of the religious iceberg in Northern Europe is getting gradually smaller – or, more precisely, is altering in shape. But this is to ignore the vast mass under the water which is invisible for most of the time, but without which the visible part would not be there at all. How, though, can a sociologist penetrate beneath the surface in order to understand what is going on underneath?

One line of approach lies in observing human behaviour (collective as well as individual) at the moments when 'normal' ways of living are, for one reason or another, suspended and something far more instinctive comes to the fore. One such occurred in Sweden in 1994, following the sinking of the Baltic ferry, *Estonia*, with the loss of some 900 lives. The shock for Swedish people, a safety-conscious nation if ever there was one, was immense; with no exaggeration the unthinkable had happened. And almost without hesitation, the Swedish people went to their churches not only to gather, to light candles and to mourn privately, but also in the correct anticipation that someone (the Archbishop) would articulate on their behalf (vicariously) both the sentiments of the people and the meaning of the tragedy. This, for the Swedish people, is precisely what the churches are for and why they should be sustained financially. The care of the Swedish Church for the victims of the Tsunami in 2004 was both similar and different. It was much less visible, but none the less took place following an event in which disproportionate numbers of Swedish people lost their lives.

Similar episodes can be found in Britain. One of the most obvious occurred after the death of Princess Diana in Paris as the result of a car crash in August 1997. Once again, large numbers of British people were drawn to their churches to make some sort of gesture. This happened in two ways: first the churches became an important, though not the only, gathering point for a wide variety of individual gestures of mourning in which Christian and less Christian symbols became inextricably mixed, both materially (candles, playing cards and madonnas) and theologically (life after death was strongly affirmed, but with no notion of judgement). More significant, however, was an awareness in the population as a whole that multiple and well-intentioned gestures of individual mourning were, in themselves, inadequate to mark the end of this particular life (as indeed of any other). Hence the need for public ritual or public liturgy, in other words a funeral, and where else but in the established church. The fact that Princess Diana had not led an unequivocally Christian life was beside the point – she, like the rest of us, had a right to the services of the Church at the end of her life. It follows that the churches must exist in order to meet such demands.[13]

Princess Diana was in fact an entirely typical English woman in terms of her religious pilgrimage (the word is chosen deliberately). She was baptized, confirmed and married in the Church of England, but then looked elsewhere – disillusioned maybe at a time of considerable unhappiness in her personal life. We know, for example, that she visited a guru and that was attracted, if only fleetingly, to Catholicism (her mother had by this time become a Catholic). And, at the end of her life, Diana was keeping company with the son of a prominent Muslim. Despite this, her funeral (effectively if not formally a state occasion) took place in Westminster Abbey, a request that the Dean and Chapter could not possibly have refused.[14] The understanding that this was a right and proper thing to do was widely shared. A religious funeral is not the prerogative of the practising or morally upright minority; they in fact were the most likely group to be critical of the whole affair.

A second and particularly poignant British example of vicarious religion took place in a small East Anglian town in August 2002. Two schoolgirls, Holly Wells and Jessica Chapman, were murdered by a school caretaker in Soham, Cambridgeshire, at the beginning of the school holidays – an episode which shocked the nation. The reaction of both the families and the community was, however, immediate. Once again they turned to the Church, personified in the form of the local vicar, who emerged as the spokesperson for both the immediate family of each child and for the population as a whole. The church building became the focus of mourning, offering both comfort and ritual as the devastated community tried to come to terms with what had happened. At the end of August a memorial service took place in Ely Cathedral. At this point, it was necessary to find a building which offered sufficient space for all those who wanted to take part (the local church no longer sufficed for even a ticket only service). Some form of closure, or at least a moving-on, was achieved, finally, as the school year re-commenced: the school community gathered on the playing field as the vicar released two white doves into the sky.

The crucial point to grasp in terms of sociological method is the need to be attentive to episodes, whether individual or collective, in or through which the implicit becomes explicit, or the abnormal normal.[15] With this in mind, it is equally important to remember that the examples outlined above are simply large-scale and media-hyped versions of what goes on all the time in the life-cycles of ordinary people. Individual families and communities regularly pause for thought at critical moments in their existence, frequently marking these with some form of liturgy. Birth (baptism) and death are the most obvious of these events, but confirmation and marriage remain significant for many in the Nordic countries. Indeed the persistence (and in some cases growth) of the occasional offices in the Lutheran parts of Northern Europe should not be overlooked in our haste to affirm institutional decline;[16] they offer important counter evidence.

So much for the continuing role of the churches in the life-cycles of European people. One quite different feature of Europe's religious life leads in a similar direction – that is, to a better understanding of vicariousness. This reflects the symbolic importance of the church building both for the community of which it is part and, in many cases, for the wider public. Few Northern Europeans attend their churches with any regularity; that is abundantly clear. Many more, however, feel strongly about the church buildings present in their locality, but only protest (make their feelings explicit) when a building is threatened with closure. The status quo is simply taken for granted until disturbed, when it becomes an issue of considerable importance. Rather more subtle, but equally revealing in this connection, are the reactions of the wider public if they are asked to pay to enter a religious building. In many ways, the usual roles are reversed. The worshipping community, burdened by the maintenance of their building are anxious both to generate income and to reduce the wear and tear caused by constant visitors; they are frequently in favour of entry charges. The wider public, in contrast, resent being asked for money on the grounds that such buildings, particularly those that belong to the historic churches, are considered public rather than private space, to which everyone (believer or not) should have the right of access. They do not belong exclusively to those who use them regularly.

Once the notion of vicariousness has been put in place, a series of sociological questions inevitably follow. It is these that I have explored in considerable detail in *Religion in Modern Europe*.[17] It is in this context that the nature (as well as the role) of Europe's historic churches becomes apparent, the more so if seen in a comparative perspective. It becomes increasingly clear, for example, that European populations continue to see such churches as public utilities maintained for the common good, not least in sustaining theologies on behalf of wider populations – a situation quite different from that in the United States. Or to put the same point in rather different terms, Europeans from all parts of the Continent understand the meaning of vicariousness (an understanding that overrides questions of translation). Explaining the concept to an American audience is, in contrast, much more difficult; quite simply it has no, or little, resonance.[18] An entirely different ecclesiastical history has led to different understandings of the relationship between Church and society, a situation accurately described as a market.

With this in mind, I am convinced that vicariousness still resonates in Europe in the early years of the twenty-first century and will do for the foreseeable future. As a concept, it is both more penetrating and more accurate than believing without belonging.[19] The longer term, however, is more difficult to predict, bearing in mind the complexities in the relationship between belief and belonging already described. A whole range of issues need to be taken into account in this respect, not least an increasingly discernible mutation in the religious lives of Europeans – from what might be called a culture of obligation to one of consumption.

From obligation to consumption

At the start of the twenty-first century, a whole set of interrelated shifts are occurring in the religious life of Europe. First, the historic churches – despite their continuing presence – are systematically losing their capacity to discipline the religious thinking of large sections of the population, especially among the young (that is abundantly clear). The latter respond, however, in complex ways – they are just as ready to experiment with new forms of belief as they are to reject the notion of belief altogether. At the same time, the range of choice is becoming wider as innovative forms of religion come into Europe from outside, largely as the result of the movement of people. Populations that have arrived in Europe primarily for economic reasons bring with them different ways of being religious (some Christian and some not). And quite apart from the incoming movements, European people travel the world, experiencing, among other things, considerable religious diversity. In this sense, a genuine religious market is emerging in most parts of the Continent.

The crucial question lies, however, not in the existence of the market in itself but in the capacities of Europeans to make use of this, the major point of contrast with the United States. Having underlined this difference many times, I am not about to change my mind. I *am*, however, beginning to wonder whether a significant and, this time, authentically European mutation might be taking place, both inside and outside the historic churches. The mutation in question takes the form of a gradual shift away from an understanding of religion as a form of obligation and towards an increasing emphasis on consumption. In other words, what until moderately recently was simply imposed (with all the negative connotations of this word), or inherited (a rather more positive spin) becomes instead a matter of personal choice. I go to church (or to another religious organization) because I want to, maybe for a short period or maybe for longer, to fulfil a particular rather than a general need in my life and where I will continue my attachment as long as it provides what I want, but I have no *obligation* either to attend in the first place or to continue if I don't want to.

If (and the question must remain tentative) such a shift is indeed taking place, what might be the implications for the patterns of religion in modern Britain? The first point to grasp, paradoxically, is that the emergent pattern is not only entirely compatible with vicariousness but to a large extent depends upon it: the churches need to be there in order that individuals may attend them if they so choose. The 'chemistry', however, gradually alters, a change in mood which is discernible in both practice and belief, not to mention the connections between them. An obvious illustration can be found in the patterns of confirmation in the Church of England. It is true that the overall numbers of confirmations have dropped dramatically in the post-war period, evidence once again of institutional decline. In England, though not yet in the Nordic countries, confirmation is no longer a teenage rite of passage (imposed by the institution) but a relatively rare event undertaken as a matter of personal choice by people of all ages. Hence the marked rise in the proportion of adult confirmations among the candidates overall – by no means enough, however, to offset the fall among teenagers.

Confirmation becomes, therefore, a very significant event for those individuals who choose this option, an attitude that is bound to affect the rite itself – which now includes the space for a public declaration of faith. It becomes in fact an opportunity to make public what has often been an entirely private activity (see below). It is increasingly common, moreover, to baptize an adult candidate immediately before the confirmation, a gesture which is evidence in itself of the fall in infant baptism some 20 to 30 years earlier. Taken together, these events indicate a marked change in the nature of membership in the historic churches which become, in some senses, much more like their non-established counterparts. Voluntarism is beginning to establish itself *de facto*, regardless of the constitutional position of the institution in question. Or to continue the chemical analogy a little further, a whole set of new reactions are set off which in the *longer* term (the stress is important) may have a profound effect on the nature of European religion.

Voluntarism can be pursued in other ways as well, not least in the choices that the religiously active appear to be making at the beginning of the twenty-first century – both are particularly evident in the British case. Here, within a constituency which is evidently reduced, two options stand out as disproportionately popular. The first is the conservative evangelical church – the success story of late twentieth-century churchgoing, both inside and outside the mainstream. These are churches which draw their members from a relatively wide geographical area and work on a congregational, rather than parish model. Individuals are invited to opt in rather than opt out, and membership implies commitment to a set of specified beliefs and behavioural codes. For significant numbers of people, these churches offer firm boundaries, clear guidance and considerable support – effective protection from the vicissitudes of life. (They run the risk, of course, of the corresponding negative attributes; more than other types of churches, they can become both excluding and exclusive.)

This is not the whole story, however. On closer inspection, it is clear that some kinds of evangelical church are doing better than others – those that incorporate a charismatic element. Old-fashioned biblicism is noticeably less popular. It is the softer charismatic forms of evangelicalism that appeal in particular to late modern populations, a suggestion strongly supported by the findings of the Kendal project.[20] The tendency is wonderfully epitomized in the *Alpha* course – a formula which brings together basic biblical teaching, warm friendship and an emphasis on the Holy Spirit. Clearly this is a winning combination; the success rates are impressive by any conventional indicator (geographical spread, the numbers of classes, throughput of customers and a growing profile in the population at large).[21] Whether you like *Alpha* or not (and many people, both inside and outside the churches, do not), it is hard to think of an equivalent movement, religious or secular, of parallel proportions.

Very different and less frequently recognized in the writing about religion in modern Britain is the evident popularity of cathedrals and city centre churches. Cathedrals, and their equivalents, deal with diverse constituencies. Working from the inside out, they are frequented by regular and irregular worshippers, pilgrims, visitors and tourists, bearing in mind that the lines between these groups are frequently blurred. The numbers are considerable – the more so on special occasions, both civic and religious. Hence the concerns about upkeep and facilities which lead in turn to difficult debates about finance (see above). Looked at from the point of view of consumption, however, cathedrals are places that offer a distinctive product: traditional liturgy, top-class music and excellence in preaching, all of which take place in a historic and often very beautiful building. A visit to a cathedral is an aesthetic experience, sought after by a wide variety of people, including those for whom membership or commitment present difficulties. They are places where there is no obligation to opt in or to participate in communal activities beyond the service itself. In this respect, they become almost the mirror image of the evangelical churches already described.

What then is the common feature in these very different stories. It is, I think, the experiential or 'feel-good' factor, whether this be expressed in charismatic worship, in the *Alpha* weekend, in the tranquillity of cathedral evensong or in a special cathedral occasion (a candlelit carol service or a major civic event). The point is that we *feel* something; we *experience* the sacred, the set apart. The purely cerebral is less appealing. Durkheim was entirely correct in this respect: for late modern populations it is the taking part that matters – and the feelings so engendered. If we feel nothing, we are much less likely to be attracted.

One further remark completes this section. It concerns the public as well as the private implications of choosing religion. Classic versions of secularization theory[22] carry with them the notion that chosen religion is necessarily privatized religion. It is an indication that the sacred canopy that used to embrace the totality of believers is no longer operative; religion has become instead a matter of lifestyle and personal preference. Prompted by discussions with sociologists in the Nordic countries, I am no longer convinced that this is so. Those who opt seriously for religion in European societies will want to make their views heard in public as well as private debate. It is at this point, moreover, that the forms of religion (both Christian and non-Christian) that have arrived more recently within Europe begin to make an effective impact: they offer positive (at times inspirational) models to the host community. A detailed discussion of the place of Islam in the religious life of Europe lies beyond the scope of this chapter; it is becoming, however, an ever more crucial factor in the overall analysis.

Concluding remarks

What then are the implications of this kind of analysis for those involved in ministry? They lie, first, in understanding better the context of which the churches are part. More precisely, they lie in an awareness that the decline in certain kinds of religious activity is part of a metamorphosis in the nature of society – a shift which has brought about the collapse in voluntary activities of all kinds. The consequences of this shift are serious for the churches, but it is not in itself the fault of those in ministry. Nor is this change in the nature of society the whole story as far as religious organizations are concerned. It is quite clear, for example, that certain kinds of churches are doing well – those that make attendance and commitment worth while for a variety of different constituencies. It is also important to remember that the 'popular' choices outlined above do not exhaust the possibilities – other forms of ministry can attract and hold congregations. The crucial point to grasp is that a sense of habit or obligation is no longer sufficient: something more is required. But that something can be extremely varied and can differ from place to place. In the chapters that follow, examples abound. The best of these combine faithful ministry – that is, an affirmation of what is already good – with a willingness to experiment. Successful innovations will be those which bring together a sensitivity to the past (parish ministry) with careful thinking about the future (how to let this ministry evolve in constructive and fruitful ways). Most certainly, it can be done.

PART TWO:
THEOLOGICAL RESOURCES

4

Theological resources for re-examining church

Rowan Williams

The first three contributors have set a context for reflection on the future of the parish system from the perspective of history, psychology and sociology. In the second part of the book the writers offer three perspectives on the theological resources we need to re-imagine church and ministry in this particular context for the twenty-first century.

Rowan Williams has been Archbishop of Canterbury since 2003. He was previously Bishop of Monmouth and before that Lady Margaret Professor of Theology in the University of Oxford. He brings many gifts to his ministry as Archbishop of Canterbury, not least, a keen theological mind and experience of and passion for exploring new life and mission through fresh expressions of church. He writes here of the need to begin to re-imagine church with the New Testament and the experience of the first Christians.

The New Testament picture

What actually happens in the New Testament? The answers probably seem obvious to most of us: the Son of God is born, lives, teaches, dies and rises; his disciples proclaim the message, and St Paul and others refine and explore the meaning of Jesus' life and death. In and around it all, communities of believers grow up under the name of 'church', *ekklesia*.

But as with any clear and obvious answers, it helps to step back a bit, in case we assume too quickly that we know just what this meant then and means now. We know roughly what we mean by 'church' and 'Son of God' and even 'disciple'. But none of these terms started out as the kind of Christian technical term we are now familiar with. It's worth asking what we can know or guess about the meaning of such language as it might have been heard by the first hearers and readers of Christian writing – the people who are addressed in Paul's letters.

One of the surprising things, of course, if you start with this sort of question, is that you realize that 'church' is a more basic idea than you might have thought. It is the audience Paul is taking for granted, the context he's writing into. There are already communities around the cities of the Mediterranean calling themselves 'citizens' assemblies' (the normal meaning of the Greek term *ekklesiai*). Sometimes it seems as though Paul is thinking about them all together as a single 'assembly of God' (1 Corinthians 10.32; 15.9).

These are groups about which – in the light of Paul's letters and some other documents – we know some things for certain. They are fairly familiar with what we call the Old Testament, though they are racially mixed. They initiate people by dipping them in water. They meet regularly for a common meal in which a loaf is broken and shared and a cup passed round in a ritual that is believed to give members of the group a share in the life of God's anointed one, Jesus. They are confused about how much of the Jewish law applies to them, and so are not clear what they can eat in common, apart from the bread and wine of the ritual meal, and how far they are bound in social contexts to observe rules about safe or pure food. They include a wide spectrum of economic status, with tensions arising as a result. Their meetings are liable to be chaotically unstructured, with a high level of eccentric behaviour. There are tensions about the role and relative status of men and women; something is clearly different about this compared with the society around, but it isn't clear what. They know by oral report something about the life and death and rising of Jesus, but as yet have no documents that bring this knowledge together. They have close relations with the senior figures who introduced them to these practices and these reports about Jesus, and this too is a source of some stress and rivalry. And they are supposed to love one another and to do all they can for each other.

Paul writes to groups that have been in existence for a while, struggling to get them to see what they are really about, what the implications are of what they are doing and hearing – implications for how they treat each other, implications for how they talk about Jesus. But *what* is it that has already happened?

The only answer that makes much sense is that the 'assemblies' are people who have been brought up to believe that their meetings with each other are meetings with Jesus; that this person, who was executed by Roman law and then encountered again alive and active, has acted now, through his friends and witnesses, to bring more and more people into his company. And by being in his company, peace with God is assured; a power is introduced into the world that makes it possible to conceive of human relations differently – as mutual service and nurture, not mutual threat – and this constitutes a foretaste of what God purposes to do and to realize in the whole universe. The death of Jesus has broken through the self-isolation of human beings from God; it has made it possible for human beings to receive the forgiveness God wants to give. But the receiving of that forgiveness is not just a matter of hearing the words. It is actual companionship with a living Jesus who gives us what we need (his 'breath', his Spirit) to pray to God the Father as he does.

The groups that thought and behaved in these ways, the groups that read Paul's challenges and speculations, were the groups that, in a couple more decades, would be reading the Gospels. They would read with some of these issues and assumptions in mind – so that they would not always read as we might naturally read now. What they would have found out in the Gospels would be something like this. Jesus had, in his teaching and actions, offered a radical and controversial answer to the question of what it takes to belong to the people of God. In contrast to the prevailing answers in his own context – loyalty to a system of ritual behaviour, managed by a governing professional class of clergy, and fidelity to the most demanding possible interpretation of holy law, managed by a governing class of lay experts – Jesus announces that the decision to trust God's will to heal and forgive creates a solidarity between people that is immeasurably stronger than the conventional bonds defining God's people. He does not attack ritual or law as such, but offers possibilities for those who have no hope of satisfactorily performing either ritual or broadly legal requirements, and so undermines the managing systems of his religious world. The outward marks of this are charismatic healing (reincorporating people into the community where God is worshipped) and indiscriminate hospitality.

It is against this background that Jesus' execution makes sense. He refuses the systems by which his world is managed and so bears the full cost of the ways in which human beings try to define themselves independently of God; he 'pays the price of sin'. But the strong emphasis on the material reality (however strangely altered) of his risen life underlines the claim that it is within *this* world, in the actual fellowship of his friends here and now, that God's work of remaking his people is first to be seen – not just in the propagation of new *ideas* about God or just in the experience of individuals. The cross and the resurrection change what is possible in *this* world as well as in the world to come.

Put this now against the wider background of the sacred books of Jesus' tradition: what is claimed there for the people of God is now claimed to apply to the assemblies of believers in Jesus. And what is defined in the holy books as the nature and task of God's people applies to these communities. They are to be witnesses to God's promise of loyalty to those he has chosen, and so to convince the world that God is to be trusted. They are to be a nation, a people, whose solidarity lies not in ethnic sameness or legal definition but in common dependence on God. They are to illuminate the world of diverse human societies by showing that there is something deeper than ordinary human solidarity – the togetherness and equality of those called and accepted by God, whose shared life now shows the world God's character. They are to witness to the fact that no sin or failure is beyond God's capacity to heal. They are to live as if in a new world, their whole mental and imaginative horizons changed – the full meaning of 'conversion'.

This, I suggest, is what's actually happening in the New Testament: the possibility of relationship with Jesus has opened up a new kind of life together, in which people discover more about the character of God as it is lived out in Jesus, and become part of the living-out of this life in their own circumstances, so as to offer hope to the world at large. The deepest theological resource for thinking about the Church now is this complex event which is laid out in the New Testament – an event which is in some sense going on now. It is going on now because the encounter is the same. Each Christian generation makes itself responsible, as did Jesus' first friends, for bringing people into relation with him and so with each other. When that happens, the Church 'happens' – and it is always helpful to think of the Church as an event before it is an institution. In what follows, I shall try to tease out a bit further what implications all this might have for the renewal of our Church now.

Using our history

It should be clear in such a model that the organizational side of the Church's life as we know it will always be secondary to and in the service of the event. This need not mean, as some people believe, that there is always an incurable tension between the 'spiritual' and the 'institutional' in the Church's life. This is a cliché – at best a half-truth, at worst an invitation to sentimentalism. The event in which people encounter Jesus as contemporary is not a timeless mystical reality, but something that is made possible by the complex web of belief and witness and human relationship connecting us to the actual events that took place in Palestine two millennia ago. To say – as we always have to –

that the real action here is that of the breath, the 'spirit', of God, is not to say that nothing historical therefore matters. God breathes life into the stuff of this world, as when the Son of God takes flesh inside his mother's body. It is not an accident that Paul calls the Church Christ's Body: Jesus acts and invites within this particular human community and its actions and words.

If we let ourselves think that what really matters is always and only some inner individual encounter here and now, we lose our hold on one aspect of the reality of Jesus – that he is actually a true part of human history and that therefore his words were heard and passed on by human beings. The effects of his actions were likewise received by bodily beings who made sense of them by repeating or imitating them so as to open the lives of others to the same judgement and the same power. The institutional life of the Church is, or ought to be, a way of taking responsibility for the truthful and (as far as possible) adequate opening up of lives by true speech and faithful action. The idea of 'orthodoxy', which some find so frightening, is really about the struggle to keep our language transparent to the truth of Jesus, resisting ways of speaking and understanding that reduce or domesticate this radical truth. So continuities are not an evil or a distraction in the Church. Knowing how to use our history, and yes, our tradition, is part of growing up as a Christian community – learning to listen to how others have listened and how others have struggled to keep their life transparent.

This is part of what Christians mean when they express concern about the 'apostolic' faithfulness of the Church. It is expressed in diverse ways. For some it is little more than the faithful and consistent reading of the Bible; for others (including Anglicans) it is the reading of Scripture within a community that has historically continuous structures – an ordained ministry that connects with the past, a readiness to be taught how to worship by the past as well as the present. Valuing the ministry of bishops, priests and deacons, and the liturgy of the Church doesn't mean slavery to the past but a readiness to bring what *we* like and what happens to suit *us* to the discernment of brothers and sisters who have been there before, and to be open to resources beyond what we now take for granted. It is one way of receiving the Spirit.

And within the context of our own local church in England, the legacy of the parochial system is part of this side of our life as Church. The model of a group of worshippers within every 'natural' community in a country, trying to let that community know what kind of God it worships and what, as a result, is possible for human beings, is a model that expresses eloquently some of the ways in which taking responsibility for passing on what has been received can happen. And maintaining such a system requires – increasingly – structures that support and (we must be honest) subsidize such a presence. If we go for a model of the Church as first and foremost an unstructured group of individual believers, with churches as self-supporting local groups that exist as and when resources can be found, we lose something – just as, of course, we lose something when the local presence of the Church is seen as provided by 'them' for 'us', the local outlet of a big company, in a way that disables or demeans local people. The reality is that, as Grace Davie has found, for a good many people the sense of encounter with Jesus can be helped, not hindered, by the tangible sense of a community of believers that is simply *there*, a sign of the sheer local availability of God, at work as always in those who have been invited to be in his company through Jesus. And for this to be a reality requires a fine balance of local initiative and commitment with broader structures and organizational patterns.

Parochial presence speaks of a relation of *loyalty* between church and society – a deeply awkward and even at times dangerous thing, because it can so easily degenerate into an uncritical acceptance of what this or that 'natural' society is comfortable with (not a problem exclusive to the parish, it should be said). But the ideal of the Church's 'availability' as a sign of God's accessibility, even the idea of a degree of cultural absorption or identification, is a necessary reminder that when the Church claims to open up a level of human solidarity, deeper and stronger than any form we know or can make for ourselves, it does not thereby simply negate or destroy those other kinds of solidarity that we live in. It is not easy to put this completely clearly, but if Christians enjoy solidarity as Christians and yet are otherwise abstract and rootless persons, we lose the sense that Christian solidarity can pick up the diverse sets of human and historical relationship in which we live and make of them a symphony of difference enjoyed and celebrated. The culturally detached Church (if there really is such an animal) not only offers no point of entry for actual human beings; it loses out on the positive tensions of diversity of style and nationality and language that make the Church a creative place to be. It loses, in fact, a dimension of what the Body of Christ actually and theologically is, by turning our eyes away from the real differences of persons and cultures from one another.

The parochial system and the world of 'emerging church' both assume that the Church must show itself credible by being where people are, literally and culturally. The Church has to be itself, has to put the solidarity of God's call and the life of the Body of Christ above other loyalties; yet it has to be itself in a way that is attractive and intelligible, recognizing all the chance factors of history and culture that will make it easier or harder to be committed to Jesus' company. People throw around the word 'sectarian' with some abandon in debates. But if it has a useful meaning, it must surely be to refer to any Christian body that so makes a virtue of its visible separateness as to leave no possibility of helping the culture or language of its environment to speak of Christ; a community where it will inevitably look as if, when you become a Christian, you become a less three-dimensional, less rooted, less historical or material human being. In fact, by saying, in effect, 'we can cope with the culture and history of this place, with this language and memory', the Church says, 'we are not threatened by human diversity; we are not competing for allegiance, as if the Church were just another kind of human solidarity'. And that generous, non-competitive approach to the cultural environment may therefore help materially in giving credibility to the claim that the solidarity of the Church is of another order entirely. It may show that the Church is not just another tribe, another interest group.

If the Church is there to tell people that God is hospitable, that Jesus' company can be shared now, and that this transforms the world of sinful and divided humanity, what it must, above all, guard against is the temptation to think of itself and present itself as a human association offering benefits on the same level as other leisure activities. It has to remember that it is the trustee of a divine initiative and invitation. When the parochial church turns into a way of giving a mild religious gloss to a culture or a local set of loyalties that are never exposed to criticism, we need new and radical 'ways of being Church' that will represent afresh the immediacy of God's call to relationship with Jesus and the tangible difference this makes. But equally when the new style of church life becomes separatist, self-sufficient, unconcerned with wider relationships in either Church or society, we need the witness of the localized, 'embedded' Church, with all its potential compromises and cultural limitations, to remind us that the separateness of the Church is not something like the occupation of a territory over and against the rest of human interests. We are taken back to the New Testament foundations of our thinking: the unity of the Church is not a reflection of any particular kind of human togetherness, racial, social, intellectual or emotional. It is the result of relationship to the one God who is manifested in the one Christ and accepted in the one baptism (Ephesians 4.5-6). Such unity as the Church *visibly* has will always result from a deeper penetration into this gift; unity of doctrine grows (as indeed Ephesians 4 overall suggests) out of the one act of trust that commits us to God and each other, and which becomes a living knowledge of Christ and what he has done.

Guarding the Church's integrity

So, to take up language used by one recent writer, there is indeed an element of 'anarchy' and of 'utopia' in the life of the Church. But because of its rootedness in actual human history, and because God has declared that the links and interrelations of human history are used by his grace to continue to make Christ contemporary, we cannot have a theory of the Church that leaves everything to local chance. The formalities of public ordained ministry ensure that certain aspects of the calling of the whole community are always realized – the calling of Christians to service, to intercession, to responsibility for oversight of each other and for guarding the community's integrity. The Church is always having to be reminded, recalled to its real nature, because its members are still in some degree living in the old world of rebelliousness and self-serving – what Paul calls the world of the 'flesh'. Ministry is there to recall us to the world of the Spirit. And, predictably, this happens in a diversity of ways (this is how the Spirit is always seen to work). Deacons, priests and bishops are not just a picturesque historical accident, a structure that could easily be replaced by a single homogenized pastoral ministry. The pity is that Anglicans have so often acted as though these orders are no more than a historical given, and haven't thought hard enough about the logic of their relation within the wholeness of the Church. And when the sensitive issue of lay people presiding at Holy Communion comes up for discussion, perhaps the question to be asked is not about the 'validity' in the abstract of such a practice, but about whether it is really true that God has left this or that community without the particular grace represented by the presbyter's ministry of presiding, of drawing together the prayers of the people into the single prayer of Jesus Christ. If God has given such grace, then the natural expression of it is in the public affirmation of this by the wider Church – in ordaining someone to take this responsibility.

But this is a technical point that needs arguing a lot further than would be possible or useful here. All I want to do is to try and hold together the manifest fact that the *substance* of the Church's life is the lived encounter with Jesus in the company of unexpected and unchosen others, and that the historical actuality of this always involves structures by which believers try to keep themselves alert and responsible to the act of God. Again, if we go back to the New Testament concepts we were looking at earlier in this chapter, we can see Paul appealing to the congregations to which he writes to be responsible in this sense. They are urged to think about the implications of what they are doing and to act, both morally and ritually, as if they really believed they were the place where Jesus was active by his Spirit. This involves discipline and order; not every spirit is to be indulged. And – to pick up a point noted above – it is not surprising if so much of this particular discussion focuses on the Lord's Supper in Paul's most sustained and far-reaching meditation on discipline and order in 1 Corinthians.

To remind ourselves: one of the most noticeable things about the community Paul is writing to in Corinth is that they have anxieties about what they can eat. They are worried and uncertain about the requirements of Jewish dietary law as it applies to the new community of believers in Jesus. Eating is one of the most significant things they are involved in because, within the Jewish tradition they inherit or are familiar with, it is a test case of faithfulness to God. Who you eat with and what you eat are marks of who, in God's presence, you are. Now the believer, whatever the complications of the food laws, is who she or he is in God's presence in virtue of the invitation given by Jesus; and that invitation is what is concretely presented in the Lord's Supper. This, in other words, is where the Church just is what it is. And what is special about the event is not the eating of special ritual food or even food prepared by ritually specified means: it is the most basic and un-special of foods, made distinctive simply because of its being received at the hands of Jesus. The special character of the meal makes no sense without the conviction of this presence and invitation.

Notoriously, early Christians had a lot of explaining to do about the apparent lack of properly 'religious' ritual in what they did (leading to the darkest suspicions about what they might be covering up by this appearance of everyday practice). And while the Lord's Supper became marked by more and more external signs of its special character (a process to which Paul's first Corinthian letter is already contributing), the central action and the elements of the meal remain in their simplicity. Indeed, what happens to the Lord's Supper is a microcosm of the problems of the Church overall. Just as the Church is not just another human interest group, so the Eucharist is not just a ritual activity competing for time and space with other religious acts that human beings perform. But also, just as the Church is inevitably a distinctive body doing distinctive things, so the Eucharist acquires those marks that set it apart from being just a repetition of ordinary social practices, which, as Paul sees in 1 Corinthians, simply reproduce the inequalities and injustices of the social life of the environment. The Eucharist is bound to be in some ways recognizably special – not just the rather chaotic and socially stratified buffet party that Paul so sharply caricatures. At the same time, it is necessarily the most prosaic of activities, a community made equal by being recipients of the same ordinary food and drink. What is needed to mark it out is not ritual elaboration – though that is historically inevitable and will need a degree of regular pruning – but a style of performance that will bring to light the invitation of Jesus as its foundation. This is food that is taken after the Scriptures have been recited, placing this action within the history of God's acts; food taken after a prayer that locates what is happening within the heavenly worship animated by the eternal Son of God; food taken (as the ritual form solidifies) in the context of a partial re-enactment of the founding event in the Upper Room. It is food that connects us with that band of disciples who ran away after the Last Supper; food that reminds us why we need the forgiveness of God; food that tell us that we live and flourish only because of the divine love that acted in the crucifixion of Jesus to rescue us. In brief, this is a meal designed to be experienced as a moment in which we are contemporary with all the dimensions of the action of God in Jesus.

So this returns us to the most basic insights of New Testament theology about the nature of the Church. The Church happens when Jesus is encountered, when the meeting of believers with one another is grasped as a meeting with him. And this does not occur by human planning, does not occur in any way that depends on human performance; it occurs when God's act of invitation is authoritatively spoken. This is what the Reformers meant by speaking of the Church as created by the Word. When Scripture is recited and we are situated clearly within the context of God's dealings with his people, when we simply stand before the living memory of Christ at table in the upper room, Christ on the cross, Christ breakfasting with his disciples, the Church is called into being. When it reflects on its actual performance in history and society, when it criticizes itself and challenges the way its structures work, the criterion must be this picture of how the Church is made by the utterance and initiative of God; and the fact of the Lord's Supper at the centre of our common life, as it has been from the beginning, is the tangible form taken by that criterion in the visible, material and historical world.

This does not of itself tell us exactly how to celebrate the Supper, how often, how elaborately – though it does provide a ground for holding to two important issues of practice. As I have already noted, it is at the very least odd to separate the leading of eucharistic worship from the ministry of the ordained presbyter who has some claim to act for the wider Church in time and space; this is an 'apostolic' event. And secondly, the Supper is most emphatically a sign of God's unconditional welcome as that welcome is realized in the history of Jesus Christ. It is tempting to treat it as something that can and should therefore be offered to all and sundry (as a good many people, especially in the USA, have recently been arguing with some forcefulness). But to separate it from the fellowship of baptized people, to treat it just as an open table for all, is to mistake the nature of its symbolism. The Supper is what establishes the community itself to be the sign of God's welcome by bestowing upon them the life and the mission of Jesus. Take away the apparent restrictiveness of limiting it to the baptized, and you lose the sense of a symbolic act that equips the community for its own distinctive mission. It becomes a general – and potentially an emotionally facile – sign of God's unlimited love, divorced from both cost and commissioning.

There are arguments still to be had about this, as will be very clear. But the point of substance is that the Lord's Supper is pre-eminently the event in which the Church as a visible group of believers touches its ground and origin in such a way as to be refreshed in its sense of what it is called to be, and what indeed it already is in relation to God's action. It is, as theologians and hymn writers have repeatedly said, the presence of the future here and now in history, and so the seed of conversion and renewal for individual and group alike.

Conclusion

If we begin from what I have suggested is the basic insight of the New Testament in our thinking about the Church – the picture of believers assembled in the company of the living Jesus, called into fellowship and equipped to call others – we have a clear touchstone for discerning what counts and what has priority in the life of the Church now. And although it is tempting to read this as a justification for sitting light to any kind of structure at all, we need not to lose sight of the importance of the claim that it is specific historical people and specific links and networks that enable the re-presentation of the news of Jesus. We are, as church, bound to find ourselves in a degree of tension between what is needed to assure this re-presentation, the patterns of public ministry that speak for the continuity and integrity of the community's witness through time, and the uncontrollable fertility of God's invitation and initiative. As we think about the pattern of the Church's life in the new millennium, we have to learn to live with this, avoiding the temptation of, on the one hand, looking for a structure-free, improvisatory community and, on the other, defining the Church simply in terms of its given patterns. The patterns – the threefold ministry, the sacramental discipline – need always to be seen in the light of the central reality, the call to Jesus' company, and understood (and criticized) in that context, so that they do not become self-perpetuating and self-serving. And it is, I have argued, the steady presence at the heart of the Church's life that is the Lord's Supper that holds all this. The ministerial structures in our common life find their expression at the Eucharist; they serve a reality they never control, the divine invitation.

Anglicanism has, historically, a good deal going for it in its conservation of the threefold order and its willingness to go on rethinking the actual embodiment of this order; in its parochial system and its readiness to offer a parish-like ministry of accessible welcome in non-parochial settings (as in its record of chaplaincy); in its sacramental theology and its tradition of improvising pastoral liturgy alongside this sacramental stream (harvest festivals and carol services, family services and national events). The weaknesses of all this are all too manifest at times – untheological opportunism, the risks of merely providing a religious accompaniment to secular events: a cosy and uncritical ethos in worship, just as likely to be found in 'experimental' as in traditional contexts. At the moment we probably need a much more robust defence of the supernatural, God-initiated side of our church life and the significance of the sacraments as actually *creating* the Church week by week. Yet, granted all this, our history offers opportunities; and our theology, biblical but shaped by the actual experience of the centuries, should help us see better how to use those opportunities. And as this happens, we find out once again the unspeakable joy of knowing Jesus as our contemporary.

5

Focusing church life on a theology of mission

Graham Cray

Graham Cray is Bishop of Maidstone and a former principal of Ridley Hall and Vicar of St Michael-le-Belfrey in York. He chaired the working party that produced Mission-shaped Church *and in this chapter develops further the theology and values that need to undergird the life of a Church when it seeks to be shaped by mission.*

Introduction

Theology lies at the heart of all church life. Anglicans (and most other Christians) believe in 'the faith uniquely revealed in the holy Scriptures, and set forth in the catholic creeds'. This inheritance of faith has immediate missionary consequence. It is to be 'proclaimed afresh in each generation'. Above all, as 'the grace and truth of Christ', it is to be brought to 'this generation', so that Christ will be known by them as well. The *Mission-shaped Church* report assumed, but did not take for granted that, 'to be missionary, a church has to proclaim afresh the faith of the Scriptures and the creeds. This is not a "value" of the Church, but the foundation upon which church is built.'

Tragically, it is possible for Christians to become so used to reciting the creeds, and hearing the lectionary passages read out, that their missionary implications are ignored. We get so used to the routine of church that the demands of church pass straight over our heads. In this chapter I will outline some of the missionary implications of our faith, as we face the challenge of proclaiming it afresh during a time of substantial cultural change.

Major cultural change presents both a danger and an opportunity. The danger is that change leaves the Church out of touch with its context and tied to inappropriate structures and patterns of ministry and mission. The opportunity is that new contexts can throw new light on Scripture and the Christian tradition and so release new resources for mission. Theology is, in many ways, the daughter of the Church's mission. It was never intended to be a detached academic exercise. It is called into being in response to the questions raised by the Church's engagement with new cultures and contexts. True Christian theology is missionary thinking for missionary action, or missionary reflection on missionary engagement.

Such thinking connects the foundational Christian truths of Scripture and the creeds to the new context being faced. As Michael Nazir-Ali has written, 'A faithful Church is continually shaped by its inner dynamic: the flow of Apostolic Tradition, with Scripture as its norm . . . The Church is, however, also shaped by the kind of world in which it finds itself. This must mean a constant receiving of the Gospel into our particular context.'[1]

The Church of England finds itself at such a time now. We are living in a major time of cultural change. Globalization, consumerism and electronic technology shape our world. Irrespective of whether academics label our time as 'postmodern' or 'late modern', there have been profound changes within modernity. Furthermore, Christendom is over. (Which is not to say that all of its heritage has disappeared.) We live in a multicultural, multi faith environment with confusing elements of secularism and spirituality.

Many of the social trends contributing to this change are outlined in chapters 1 and 2 of the *Mission-shaped Church* report. It is these new social realities which contribute to the challenges which now face the parochial system.

Bishop Michael's comment identifies the three partners in this process: the historic gospel, the contemporary world and the Church which has to 'receive the gospel again' into that context if it is to embody it faithfully. In other words there is a theological task to be attempted. To focus church life on a theology of mission is not to pretend that that task begins with a blank sheet of paper. The task is not to combine theology with social analysis and come up with an ideal Church from scratch. The task is to engage gospel (and Church) as we now know it, with culture, as it has become, to answer the question, where do we go from here?

Mission-shaped Church never attempted a full-blown, integrated theology of mission. Rather, it identified a number of the most important theological anchor points: the mission of God, mission after the pattern of Christ, the community of the Spirit, the Church as a community created to reproduce, and the classic marks of the Church according to the Nicene Creed. This chapter will revisit these themes.

In a time of change local churches will be tempted to avoid this theological challenge. The easiest way to do so is to take a short cut, and quickly settle on an existing model for church. Either they recommit themselves determinedly to the 'parochial model' – by which they mean the parish church as they have known it: because it is 'Church of England'. Or they select 'cell church', or some other model of 'fresh expression' from chapter 4 of *Mission-shaped Church*; off the shelf as it were. This split is understandable but confused. Fresh expressions of church are often an enriched way of being the parish church, and ministering to a greater range within the parish community. Cell church is used by a significant number of parish churches. Fresh expressions also help us to reach the many networks which pay no respect to parish boundaries, but they are not an either/or with the traditional model. Only an integrated and thought through partnership can serve our nation with the gospel. 'The brightest hope for church after Christendom is a symbiotic relationship between inherited and emerging churches. We need each other.'[2]

The theological task requires us to put the values of a missionary Church ahead of models of church, whether inherited or emerging.[3] The models listed in *Mission-shaped Church* were only ever intended as an accessible way to categorize the range of expression of church that we had identified by the time we went to press. They were not intended to be a complete list. Some were well established, some still at an experimental stage. Our hope was that they would encourage further missiological creativity, by stimulating the church's imagination, as much as provide working models for others to use.

When we attempted some theological assessment it quickly became clear that our models could not be judged for appropriateness apart from their local context. Was 'cell church', for example, the best and most adequate model to reach the community that a particular parish or church planting team had in view? Because the local context was so critical for any form of mission-shaped church, we developed a list of five values that we would hope to see embodied, whatever the model. In our report they come at the end of the list of models for church, just before the theological chapter.[4] In practice they embody most of the key points from the theological chapter. They are applicable to both traditional and fresh ways of being church. A practical way of focusing the life of any church around a theology of mission would be to use the five values as a plumb line, a good health check, or as a list of aspirations. One warning however: like the fruit of the Spirit, where there are nine virtues but only one fruit, these five values belong together. They are an

63

attempt to identify the DNA of church, when viewing it from a mission perspective.[5]

A missionary Church is focused on the Trinity

To focus our congregational life around mission to the world, we have to begin with God. It is of the essence of the Church on earth to be a missionary community, because it is the creation of a missionary God. Our credal statements about God only exist because the Father sent the Son in the power of the Holy Spirit. They, and we, are a consequence of the divine mission. Worship lies at the heart of a missionary Church, as a response of gratitude for God's grace and goodness. Because we worship a missionary God we cannot attend to mission without attending to worship, and we cannot attend to worship without attending to mission. At their best they are both instinctive reflexes in response to the gospel, which we turn into disciplined actions. Each is the test of the integrity of the other.

The tension that often exists between these two dimensions of church life lies at the heart of many church's difficulties in becoming mission-shaped. Culture wars about the relationship between worship and mission reveal a theological inadequacy. The same gospel, which wins us as worshippers, calls us as missionaries. Once this is grasped by a congregation, and embodied in its DNA, mission becomes a call to worship, and worship becomes inseparable from witness and is expressed in hospitality to newcomers – to strangers.

A mission-shaped church will not reduce its worship to a lowest common denominator. Once (and if) it is sufficiently welcoming for seekers and those who are not yet Christians to feel safe at its services, its most powerful witness will be its worship – worship that is a full-blooded encounter with the triune God. Such an encounter is possible irrespective of churchmanship, tradition or style. How else will newcomers and guests understand how serious we are about the God we worship? How else will we be transformed to go to his world with his grace and truth? At the same time, as we shall see, all decisions about the style and culture of worship will be made to ensure that no unnecessary cultural obstacles are put in the way of those who do not yet follow Christ. There is a substantial difference between the need for new or restored Christians to learn the art and disciplines of worship, which takes time, and the maintenance of a religious environment which also requires people to change their culture to become Christians! This situation can no longer be acceptable in the Church of England.

Just to state the symbiotic relationship between mission and worship is not to solve all the problems involved in holding the two in creative tension, but a church which is clearly committed to both, and knows why, need not go far wrong. This perspective emphasizes the vital connection between mission and spirituality. Both worship and mission are ultimately for God, not for ourselves. We do not worship because we like the tradition or style, nor do we evangelize for the sake of the numbers in our churches. These activities are both from God and for God. To love and know God as Father, Son and Spirit is the chief inspiration and primary purpose of a mission-shaped Church.

All of this implies that there will be a greater emphasis on the Church as a movement, and as a community of disciples, and less on church as an institution, to the extent that an institution is taken to imply a reluctance about change.

Because the church's mission is to participate in the mission of God, all of its life and activity needs to be undergirded by prayer. This sort of mission does not presume upon previous experience. It dare not assume that what worked before will work again, nor that what worked ten years ago still ought to work now. Mission is partnership with God and it understands intercessory prayer as the primary form of partnership with God. Many of its initiatives will be birthed in prayer, and the ministry of intercession will be nurtured and honoured. Such churches will be as creative in their prayer as in their corporate worship and their missionary activities. If mission really is 'seeing what God is doing and joining in', churches will need to developing new skills of discernment. It may be that the skills of spiritual direction will need to develop in new ways as a form of mission accompaniment.

The Church is apostolic. It bears the faith delivered to the apostles and shares in their call to make it known. That is why it must be mission-shaped. 'Mission must be one of the authentic marks of the church.'[6]

A missionary Church is incarnational

Mission that is understood as sharing in the mission of God has to come to terms with the Incarnation. When 'the Word became flesh', he became culturally clothed flesh. Universal salvation was offered through a particular culture, not through a culture-free 'everyman'. The great New Testament struggle concerning the requirements made of Gentile Christians (which decided that they should not be circumcised and did not have to keep all of the Law) demonstrates once and for all that conversion to Christ does not require taking on the culture of the missionaries. Throughout its history the Church has struggled to accept this, but the challenge remains.

The pivotal section in the *Mission-shaped Church* report is its teaching on inculturation.[7] The missionary advance of Christianity has always involved the crossing of cultures and developing skills of translation.[8] 'The eternal word' really 'only speaks dialect.'[9] The one gospel wears many clothes – which means that missionaries may have to change theirs!

A church which has grasped this principle actively seeks ways to embody the gospel in ways of life, service and worship which are locally appropriate. Their primary concern is to embody Jesus (to be the Body of Christ) within the local culture or cultures. This does not mean making Jesus accessible by removing every part of his message that people find difficult or costly. But it does mean making Jesus, with all his challenge, understandable within their world and world view. It aims to face people with the real Christ, in their own culture and language, with no hint of a suggestion that to follow him should mean leaving behind their own culture and language, rather than having it transformed.

A missionary church seeks to shape itself in relation to the culture in which it is located or to which it is called, while being equally committed to remaining faithful to the gospel which it has received. This tension between relevance and syncretism lies at the heart of the relationship between the Church and the world. Churches which are aware of it regularly check whether the ways in which they live, worship and witness are making the gospel unnecessarily distant, strange or culturally irrelevant to those around them. At the same time they ask whether the gospel they seek to embody and share is still recognizably the scriptural gospel. Churches that are not aware of this tension may be engaging perfectly with their contexts. But they are not checking! It is just as likely that their life as a church has become either culturally strange, maintaining a way of life which no longer exists elsewhere in society, or they have lost all Christian distinctiveness, and appear merely to be a religious version of the rest of society.

Because the gospel can only come in cultural clothes the inculturation process can become an experience of exchange and mutual learning. Encounter with people 'not like us' puts our own culture into new perspective. For example, as Ann Morisy argues (in Chapter 9), those who have only known comfortable middle-class Britain often understand the teaching of Jesus in a new way, when they work among the poor. When we see Christ at work in situations different from our own we have the opportunity to see and be enriched by new dimensions of the gospel.

When St Paul says that Christ's Church 'is his body filling everything in every way' (Ephesians 1.23), he implies that the fullness of Christ will only be seen in his Church when the gospel is embodied in all the cultures of the earth. The implication is that we have a continual calling to go to where people are, and to plant churches which are shaped in relation to their culture, but which reflect Christ. In our current context in the UK this will often mean prioritizing our outreach towards the majority who are non-churched.

Whenever a church is called to be cross-cultural, or to church plant cross-culturally, then its long-term members or the initial team for a new project have to be willing to lay aside their own cultural preferences about church, to allow the emergence of a form of church shaped in partnership with those they are seeking to reach. Perhaps the most challenging sentence in *Mission-shaped Church* is this. 'No serious attempt at inculturation by the Church of England can begin with a fixed view of the outward form of the local church.'[10] This is costly. We used the expression 'dying to live'. This draws us from Christ's Incarnation to his cross. None of us is called to lay down our life for the salvation of others, but we, for whom Christ laid down his life, may well have to lay down much that is loved and familiar, and not wrong in itself, to reach those who are far from God. Inculturation means that the shape of the missionary congregation's life emerges from the encounter between the gospel which the missionaries carry, and the culture of those to whom they carry it.

If a church is long-established, then it regularly re-evaluates itself in relation to the culture of the community it serves, and should be prepared to strip away whatever is not required by the gospel that would put an additional obstacle in the way of others finding faith.

All of this may seem foreign to many parish congregations. But the fact is that the culture of many parish churches has become foreign to large parts of their communities. The lessons learned in other parts of the world, where Christianity has no long history, need now to be applied to Britain. This is not merely a matter of a multicultural society. It applies to any parish that has lost touch with dimensions or generations of its community. 'The issue is not relevance as far as the Church is concerned. The issue is incarnation. When so called "traditional" churches are out of touch with the people who live around them, the problem is not that they are irrelevant, but that they are not incarnational.'[11]

The incarnation requires us to take our particular community, in all its layered complexity, seriously. In this light, plans for mission will not be made on the basis of vague assumptions or guess work, nor on the basis of something which we heard had worked elsewhere. A proper audit will be done, to ensure that the local church does not end up 'saying all of the right things, but not saying them to anyone.'[12] There are many good resources that have worked elsewhere and which may be appropriate for us, but without a proper audit, we will never know.

We are not left alone with this task. An incarnational Church seeks to be responsive to the activity of the Spirit in its community. Just as the Spirit prepared the way for the coming of Christ, so we may expect God the Spirit to prepare the way for us. The Spirit may well be preparing open doors or bridges for the gospel, if we have the eyes to see, and, more importantly, the will to go.

Inculturation is important because the Church is catholic. As Paul Avis has written: 'Catholicity refers to the universal scope of the church as a society instituted by God in which all sorts and conditions of humanity, all races, nations and cultures, can find a welcome and a home. Catholicity therefore suggests that the church has the capacity to embrace diverse ways of believing and worshipping, and that this diversity comes about through the "incarnation" of Christian truth in many different cultural forms which it both critiques and affirms. The catholicity of the church is actually a mandate for cultural hospitality.'[13] This linking of inculturation with catholicity opens the way for a principled diversity in styles of church. For our diverse consumer culture will never be reached by a single standardized form of church; Church of England or not.

A missionary Church is transformational

A missionary church exists for the transformation of the community that it serves, in the light of the kingdom of God. This comes through the power of the gospel and of the Holy Spirit. Transformation is an important, unifying theme for the church's mission. Through the gospel of his Son, God transforms the eternal destiny of those who believe. People may experience conversion as a process – most people do, even where there is also a moment of clear decision. They may find that their unfocused childhood belief becomes focused into a clear commitment. They may have no history with the Christian faith at all prior to the events that led to their conversion. But whatever their personal experience, theologically, within that process, God makes them new and brings them from death to life, from darkness to light.

The gospel is also the power of God for the transformation of our lifestyle. Growth in faith in Christ is also the means of growth in Christ-likeness – Christ being formed in us.

This personal transformation is part of something much bigger. Christians look forward with confidence to a new heaven and a new earth. They know that what began with the resurrection of Christ, through the power of the Holy Spirit, will be completed when Christ appears, by the transformation of the whole creation. This does not mean universal salvation. The Bible says clearly that at that time there will be a final judgement. But is does mean that the world will not end but be transformed.

Through Christ, in this life, we may see anticipations of that transformed universe. 'It is a vital part of a Christian perspective on this world to identify within it scattered acts of recreative anticipation of God's promised future, as the same Spirit who raised Jesus from death calls into being life, health, faith and hope where there is otherwise no capacity for these and no accounting for them. Such anticipations are to be found in this world, but they are not of this world. They belong to God's future of which they are heralds and towards which they direct our hopeful gaze.'[14]

The Holy Spirit brings the power of the future world into the present world. Personal salvation is experiencing the great acquittal of the last day in advance. Transformation of character is an anticipation of the day when we will be fully like Christ. 'I am determined by the future God has promised rather than by the past I have made.'[15] In the same way, through the power of the Spirit we may reasonably hope for imperfect transformations in our communities and in the environment. 'The Holy Spirit brings forward a reality which is grounded in divine promise rather than in human thought or achievement.'[16]

Churches that grasp this vision see everything and everyone in the light of the future world. Their attitude is not that it is not worth seeking change in their communities because they cannot last, but to treat everything on the basis of its capacity to last forever.

In the Christian vision, imperfect and incomplete transformations, whether personal or communal, are steps towards a promised future. Jesus' name for this promised future was the kingdom of God. He taught that it was already present through his ministry, as well as coming fully in the future. If Christians have been reborn into his kingdom and share his vision, their churches cannot be self-serving, self-seeking or self-focused. Rather they are to be communities of hope. The kingdom of God is their goal, and church is understood as a servant and sign of God's kingdom in their communities, whether those individual communities are based in a neighbourhood or a network.

Churches like this have no unresolved tension between evangelism and social action. They are active in their communities in the light of the kingdom, for the sake of the kingdom and seeking new citizens for the kingdom.

The Church is holy. It is set aside for God's purposes in this world, in the light of what will be, because God promises a renewed world. Holiness is not about withdrawal from the world, but about committed distinctiveness for the sake of the world. The Church is a community that anticipates God's future as least as much as it conserves its own history.

A missionary Church makes disciples

A missionary church is active in calling people to faith in Jesus Christ. It has no embarrassment or shame about this activity, but it does treat each person with dignity and sensitivity, and avoids any manipulation. All of this is for one reason. Every individual is a person for whom Christ died.

Any church that has been grasped by the gospel will want to establish access pathways for new people to move towards faith, with understanding and commitment. The embarrassment about evangelism, which still impedes far too many in the Church of England, needs to be overcome. Even in secular terms, people expect a garage to offer them cars and a clothing shop to offer them clothes. Why then would they not expect a church to offer them Christ? Both insider and outsider might have been put off by bad practice, but the way to correct bad practice is to teach good practice, of which much is available.

But there are theological reasons for faith sharing. Just as worship is a response to God's extraordinary generosity, so faith sharing is an extension of that generosity by offering it to others. Evangelism is part of the economy of grace. Freely you have received, freely give. 'Bring the grace and truth of Christ to this generation.'

Evangelism should not be thought of in isolation, or seen as a distinct discipline, but as a key component of disciple making – which is a lifelong process. Missionary churches are not so much looking for prayers of

70

commitment but for lifelong commitment. They are equally committed to the development of a consistent Christian lifestyle appropriate to, but not withdrawn from, the culture or cultures in which they operate.

Disciple making is the missing component of many churches. Where are the intentional programmes and spiritual disciplines designed to help Christians to reach the point where they act in a Christ-like way in every aspect of their lives? The growth of disciples is a central calling of the local church. In practice it will involve some pattern of discipleship groups, allowing each Christian who is serious about discipleship, to have a place of mutual support and accountability.

This is particularly important now that we inhabit an individualistic consumer culture. In the introduction to *Mission-shaped Church* I wrote: 'It is the incarnation of the gospel, within a dominantly consumer society that provides the Church of England with its major missionary challenge.'[17] Local churches need to be communities that enable their members to live in a consumer society, but not to be of (shaped by) the values of a consumer society. We cannot escape a consumer culture and continue to be missionaries here. But local churches face the challenge of demonstrating an alternative to consumerism from within it.

Once again, an understanding of the Incarnation and the cross helps to show the necessity of distinctive discipleship. Christ's consistent faithfulness to the Father took him to the cross. A life shaped by Christ's Incarnation is inherently counter-cultural, in that it aims at faithful Christian discipleship within the new context, rather than cultural withdrawal or cultural conformity. The gospel has to be heard within the culture of the day, but it always has to be heard as a call to appropriate repentance. This does not conflict with God's love. In love God sent his Son so that we need not perish! A truly missionary church engages with its culture, but also presents a counter-cultural challenge by its corporate life, and the personal lives of its members.

There is a direct connection between whole-life discipleship and evangelism. Lives that consistently display Christ create hunger for Christ in others. Evangelism without discipleship borders dangerously on hypocrisy.

But discipleship is about more than character formation and consistency. It is also about gifting and ministry. A missionary Church encourages the gifting and vocation of all the people of God. All Christians share in ministry. For too long 'spiritual gifts' have been regarded as primarily internal resources to maintain the church in its religious activities. But Paul teaches that gifts are to be used for building up, both inside and out the church (1 Corinthians 10.23; 14.12), or it would be better to say, in the ministry of the Church when it is gathered and when it is scattered. A missionary Church does not pretend that every member is an evangelist. Rather it helps every member to identify and mature in the use of the gifts God has given them, for the whole of life. 'In exercising spiritual gifts, we are involved in the restoration of God's perfect work in creation. An activity can only be characterized as a spiritual gift when it assists in the restoration of creation and contributes to the restoration of a sick world.'[18]

Finally, disciple-making churches invest in the development of leaders. Leadership is not seen as a restricted area to be guarded, but a priority area to be multiplied. Hopefully, good leaders are looking for those who might prove to be better leaders than they are. With a view to the diversity of the mission field they are also looking for potential leaders who are not like them, who might help them cross cultures and develop fresh expressions of church. Cross-cultural missionaries want the next generation of leaders to be indigenous, and make it a priority to discover and mentor them. My suspicion is that many churches decline because of a lack of imaginative investment in leadership development.

A missionary Church is relational

The final value for a missionary Church, a Church whose life is wrapped around a theology of mission, is that it is a community. Faith is understood as personal, but not individual. Christianity is understood to be, and experienced as, essentially corporate. Believers do not so much 'go' to church as 'be' church. Sometimes, they are church gathered, sometimes, they are church scattered. A community of faith is being formed.

In part this returns us to issues addressed earlier. A missionary church is characterized by welcome and hospitality. Hospitality is seen as the ethical counterpart to witness. Witness is closely linked to welcome. But this is more than an initial welcome. Churches like this expect to be changed by new members because an interdependent community is being formed.

Believers are encouraged to establish interdependent relationships with their fellow believers as they grow into Christ. A primary purpose of these relationships, as we have seen, is mutual support for growth in discipleship. This is because a primary purpose of church gathered is to equip each member for life as part of the church scattered. But there is also a deeper theological reason. We are created in the image of the Triune God. We are made for relationships. Furthermore, Christ died to reconcile us back to God and to one another. The social consequences of all this have been beautifully stated by Jürgen Moltmann. 'I am free and feel myself to be free, when I am recognized and accepted by others and when I, for my part, recognize and accept others. I become truly free when I open my life for others and share it with them, and when others open their lives for me and share their lives with me. Then the other person is no longer a limitation on my freedom but the completion of it.'[19] This is the sort of community for which we were created and for which Christ died. As such, it demonstrates the life of Christ to the world and nurtures and sustains each disciple. It is not that any church is perfectly like this, but it is the God-given goal.

This fundamental commitment to corporateness and mutuality is also to be expressed between churches. As a community, a missionary church is aware that it is incomplete without interdependent relationships with other Christian churches and communities. It does not think it is the whole answer to any mission field, local community or missionary challenge. It knows it is incomplete by itself and never seeks to stand alone. The language of a mixed economy of church life, of a coherent partnership between traditional models of church and fresh expressions of church, has profound theological grounding. In a study on the missionary implications of the letter to the Ephesians, Andrew Walls wrote, 'The Ephesian metaphors of the temple and of the body show each of the culture-specific segments as necessary to the body but as incomplete in itself. Only in Christ does completeness, fullness, dwell. None of us can reach Christ's completeness on our own. We need each other's vision to correct, enlarge and focus our own; only together are we complete in Christ.'[20] A missionary Church has a healthy humility. It knows that it is not the whole answer!

The Church is one through baptism. Within that unity is room for substantial diversity. That diversity can be doctrinal, within the boundaries set by the creeds that we share. It can most certainly be cultural. But visible local respect, mutuality and trust is vital for the missionary work of the Church to thrive.

Much more could be said about a missionary Church. These five principles provide a broad standard to help discernment at a time when the shape of the Church of England is increasingly varied and in flux. None of these qualities is automatically guaranteed by particular structures of mission or strategies for church or church planting. Neither do any of these qualities automatically flow from a particular church tradition or 'type'. These five marks are not 'pass' or 'fail' criteria, but may be a helpful way of highlighting or identifying a church's missionary purpose and qualities. As I mentioned at the start of this chapter, these principles can be applied to either existing or fresh expressions of church.

6

Serving, sustaining, connecting: Patterns of ministry in the mixed economy Church

Steven Croft

Steven Croft was appointed Archbishops' Missioner and Team Leader of Fresh Expressions in 2004. He was previously Warden of Cranmer Hall and before that in parish ministry in Enfield and Halifax. He is the author of a number of books including Transforming Communities *(2002) and* Learning for Ministry *(2005).*

The mixed economy Church

In order to respond to God's call and God's mission at the present time the Church of England is attempting to develop what Rowan Williams has called a mixed economy church. Hundreds of fresh expressions of church are already being developed alongside and within the parish system and many more are planned. New posts are being created in dioceses either to establish fresh expressions of church or to support fresh expressions in different ways. The Church of England is seeking to develop new structures for ministry and training for this mixed economy.

At the same time, in many parts of the country, we face reductions in the number of stipendiary posts with fewer clergy, as it seems, called to take on more responsibility. How are we to develop and structure ordained and licensed ministries in order to help establish and sustain each part of this mixed economy? What understanding of ministry do we need to support these changes? These questions are the focus of this chapter but we begin first by looking at three distinct but essential tasks.

Sustaining and developing traditional churches

We need traditional churches that are able to sustain the Christian life and witness of their present congregation and that are also able to reach out to those who have a Christian background somewhere in their past and share faith with them. These churches have a large and important mission field. According to every piece of research, these traditional churches are still able to connect with a large proportion of the population. All our traditional churches need to be nurtured, encouraged, enabled to welcome others, to reach out, to develop and grow.

Over the last decade most traditional churches have begun to engage with the call to become more mission-centred and mission-shaped. That call has generated an agenda for change and development in every congregation. How do we make our services more welcoming? How do we seek to encourage, equip and enable every-member ministry? How do we seek the transformation and renewal of our wider society? How do we nurture all ages in faith? There have been many books and studies encouraging the growth of the traditional parish church and Robin Gamble (see Chapter 7) presents a passionate argument that this way forward is both possible and vital.

Developing fresh expressions of church

The research presented in *Mission-shaped Church*, and the experience of many clergy and lay ministers, reveals that although traditional churches are still able to reach into a large proportion of the population, there are still many who are no longer able to connect. The estimates vary according to different pieces of research.

The *Mission-shaped Church* report itself argued that about 40 per cent of the population are still able to connect with traditional churches in different ways other than through occasional offices.[1] More recent studies have revealed that this proportion is itself declining and is currently more likely to be around 35 per cent, simply because a higher proportion of older people have some church background.[2]

We also need, therefore, to be actively encouraging and supporting many different fresh expressions of church in every place. These fresh expressions of church are seeking to see the gospel established in many different cultures and communities which no longer seem able to connect with the Church in its traditional form. *Mission-shaped Church* gives many stories and examples. There are many more on the fresh expressions web site (www.freshexpressions.org.uk).

There is already an immense variety of fresh expressions of church and of the ministries that support them. The whole Church is attempting to learn how to establish fresh expressions. Both Michael Moynagh (Chapter 8) and George Lings (Chapter 10) draw attention in different ways to the challenges this presents.

Connecting everything together

The mixed economy is already a reality in many parts of the country and this sense of variety and diversity will increase over the next decade. We therefore face a third task alongside the call to make every church mission-shaped and to establish fresh expressions of church. We need to connect everything together into one community. There must be unity as well as diversity because we are all part of the one Body of Christ. The fresh expressions of church need to be connected to the whole of the Christian tradition and the Church worldwide. The most traditional of congregations needs to be connected with the cutting edge. This ministry of connection is vital if fresh expressions are to remain part of the Church of England as a whole and not spin off into their own denomination as has happened so often in the past. It is also vital for the traditional Church to have the life and vitality of the new mission movements.

So, how are we to structure our patterns of ordained and recognized ministries in order to embrace these three distinct tasks of establishing fresh expressions of church; sustaining mature congregations and connecting the whole together?

Building on a sure foundation: baptism, discipleship and ministry

This chapter focuses discussion on ordained and licensed lay ministries within and beyond the life of the church. It focuses here because the way in which we think of and develop these ministries over the next decades is vital for the life and health of congregations and the witness of the whole Christian community. But this focus is only possible and desirable within the understanding that all baptized Christians are called to discipleship and ministry in the whole of their lives. Every part of who we are and what we do, all of our gifts, are to be offered to God in grateful response to all that we have received in Christ. The ministry of every Christian through their work, as volunteers, among their family and friends is all to be valued and developed.

This sense of whole-life ministry and discipleship has been rightly recaptured and re-emphasised in many ecumenical documents on ministry in recent years. In the language of the classic text in Ephesians 4, the purpose of the ordering of ministry *within* the Church is to enable and equip the people of God for ministry and mission *beyond* the Church:

> The gifts he gave were that some should be apostles, some prophets, some evangelists, some pastors and teachers, to equip the saints for the work of ministry, for the building up of the body of Christ, until all of us come to the unity of the faith and of the knowledge of the Son of God, to maturity, to the measure of the full stature of Christ.
>
> (Ephesians 4.11-13)

Learning to see in three dimensions

At first glance, the way in which the Church of England orders its ministry does not seem well suited to post-Christendom. We have focused on a stable priesthood, traditionally seen as exercising a multi-faceted ministry with a flat structure overseen by a relatively small number of bishops. We have generated a large number of different licensed lay ministries and continue to do so. We have made space to accommodate self-supporting ministry offered not only by those who are lay but also by the ordained. With some exceptions, most of these ordained and lay ministries have been directed towards supporting the parish system as it now is and the traditional Church. Where is the space and the capacity for mission, for fresh expressions and the mixed economy? Do we have to develop new categories and concepts for ministry in order to facilitate this change?

It is not surprising, therefore, that over the last two decades there have been attempts to abandon the Church of England's traditional language about ministry. These have been directed in at least two different directions.

In the first place, certain sections of the Church have tried to coin a new language for ministry, borrowed from secular life and the social sciences, and have made great use, in particular of the term 'leader'[3] as a default word for 'minister'. There are some good reasons for this. In a time of change and of new ventures it is very important to recognize the role of good leadership in enabling change and beginning new ventures. As Christians, there are many good things we can learn from the secular leadership traditions, and the notion of leadership is very much in vogue in other institutions.[4]

However, there are also some dangers in this approach. The term 'leader' is not closely connected and rooted in the Christian tradition nor the Anglican language of ministry. Christian reflection on ministry must be rooted, above all, in the person and work of Christ who came as a servant and who commends and exemplifies self-giving love and surrender of power and authority. There are many different warnings in the Gospels on the language of leadership being adopted uncritically by God's people.

Others have attempted to renew our understanding of ministry by reaching back into Scripture and the Christian tradition and arguing for a restoration of a more distinctively New Testament pattern (as they see it). In particular, they argue, there is a need to restore the range of ministries in Ephesians 4 back to the life of the local church in a post-Christendom era. We need to focus again on the gifts of apostles, prophets and evangelists (understood as ministries in the life of the Church) alongside those of pastor and teacher.

This is a serious argument, rooted in the Pentecostal and charismatic traditions and finding a voice within some sections of the Church of England. In an age when God is renewing the Church by the power of the Spirit, do we not need (and should we not expect) these dynamic, charismatic gifts and ministries to be made available once again to the churches?

But, again, for me, there are some difficulties. First, it is by no means absolutely clear what Ephesians 4 means by the terms apostles and prophets. Is this genuinely an unambiguous reference to ministries exercised within the churches to which the letter was written? We know that both men and women were described as apostles and prophets in the New Testament Church. Or is the passage looking back to *the* apostles and *the* prophets, whose ministry is for all time, alongside the ministry of evangelists, pastors and teachers, whose ministry is needed in every generation. There is evidence through the New Testament period of a development from the more general use to the restriction of the word apostle to a very limited number of founding members of the churches. It is not easy to determine where Ephesians 4 comes in this progression but the majority of commentators read this passage alongside the references in Ephesians 2 and argue for a more restricted interpretation.[5]

Secondly, we have to ask the question: If these ministries were so vital in the life of the Early Church, why were they not continued through the first three centuries of missionary expansion? It is not that they were abandoned at the conversion of Constantine at the birth of Christendom. We actually find only limited references to apostles and prophets exercising a ministry in the life of the Church after the New Testament period. Nor is this the dominant, normative tradition of ministry even within the New Testament churches. Surely this is because, with the passage of time, the Church wanted to accord a distinctive role to the apostles and prophets (and eventually, evangelists) of the Old and New Testaments and so developed alternative terms for its own ministry. This was not to deny that God would bless the Church with those who had gifts like the apostles or the prophets of the New Testament Church, simply that those *titles* should only be used in the most particular of circumstances.

The answer to the development of ministry for a mission-shaped Church lies not therefore in borrowing the language of leadership nor in recovering the terms coined and used in Ephesians 4 (though these remain vital and useful as a separate and helpful tradition) but, I want to argue, in exploring the three concepts which still lie beneath the terms we use for ordained ministry in the Church of England. These terms are deeply rooted in the oldest Christian traditions and securely anchored in our understanding of Christ. They run through every part of the Scriptures. Although they are not used in the same way in the developing New Testament tradition, by the end of the New Testament period they have together become the bearers of a Christian theology of ordained ministry. They have served the worldwide Church very well in that capacity, both through Christendom and in times of missionary expansion and development.

The three groups of words are the term *diakonia*, meaning service, from which we take the term deacon; the term *presbyteros*, meaning elder, from which we (eventually) derive the term presbyter or priest; and the term *episcope* (pronounced episcopay), watching over, from which we take the term bishop. It is clear from a number of passages in the New Testament that these are terms that emerge only gradually as the Christian community 'tries on' a number of concepts and patterns for ministry. Only at the end of the New Testament period are the three terms used in ways that are similar to the developing threefold ministry of the next century. In Acts, the three terms are used deliberately by Luke with a blurring of distinctions in the great speech to the Ephesian presbyters of Acts 20. In the Pastoral Epistles, we receive criteria for the appointment of *diakonoi* and the *episcopos*. The Pastorals also refer clearly to *presbyteroi*, apparently working collaboratively with these other ministries.

I argued in *Ministry in Three Dimensions*[6] that these three orders of ministry should helpfully be seen as describing not only three distinct orders but also three dimensions of the ministry of all of the ordained. The approach is one

80

which has been well received, in particular in helping a variety of people to make sense of their own ministries. In the same book, I also traced the biblical origins and something of the history of the different terms and ministry in the life of the churches. In 2004, as part of a sabbatical study, I had the opportunity to undertake further work on the concept of *episcope*.[7] Over the last four years I have also explored further the New Testament understanding of *diakonia*, particularly through engaging with the work of John Collins.[8]

Over the last year, as part of my reflection on the development of the mixed economy Church, I have kept on coming back to the ideas lying beneath the Anglican concept of the threefold ministry. I have become convinced that they have a great deal to commend them in terms of the needs of the Church in the present generation and, in particular, on the outworking of the three tasks outlined at the beginning of this chapter.

Deacons: servants and ambassadors creating new communities; sowers of the word

Over the last decade or so there has been a lively debate within the worldwide Church on the correct interpretation of the biblical material on *diakonia* and deacons. The inherited understanding roots the term firmly in the biblical concept of service, waiting at tables. It is therefore connected to Jesus' own call to service and, through Philippians, to the central ideas of the Incarnation as a pattern for ordained ministry. The appointment of the seven in Acts 6 is seen as the appointment of practical stewards who undertake administrative tasks on behalf of the apostles. The seven are not actually called *diakonoi* but the Greek term is used deliberately by Luke three times within this short passage. The understanding of the ministry of deacons, which derives from this reading of the New Testament, is concerned with a quiet hidden service as the foundation for all Christian ministry; with the undertaking of practical and administrative tasks; with the stewardship of resources and, in particular, the care of the poor. This understanding also lies at the foundation of the idea that the deaconate is an appropriate first stage in preparation for being ordained priest (still the case in the Church of England though not in some of our partner churches). Ordination as deacon is not cancelled, of course, through ordination as priest or bishop but this serving ministry continues alongside other ministry. All ordained ministry therefore has a foundation of service and a connection with the service of Christ.

This interpretation has been challenged by an alternative but complementary reading advanced by John Collins. His ideas are still not widely known or understood within the Church of England, primarily because they depend on a re-reading of the use of the Greek terms, not only in the New Testament, but in a variety of other ancient sources.[9] Collins argues that alongside this core meaning of service in the Greek term, the *diakonos* in the ancient world was a person of considerable authority and a recognized office bearer, an ambassador on behalf of a particular person or community.

This understanding makes excellent sense of the New Testament material. If the term *diakonos* simply means servant, are not all Christians called to this kind of service? Why single out some as representative office holders? The seven of Acts 6 are, Collins argues, clearly appointed to some kind of recognized ministry on behalf of the wider community. We actually never read about them waiting at tables. We do, however, immediately see Stephen and Philip acting as ambassadors and representatives, speaking on behalf of the community. We also see Paul referring to himself as *diakonos* and designating a number of others in this way.[10]

From all of this a picture emerges of the *diakonos* as a recognized minister acting on behalf of the wider community but beyond that wider community. Undoubtedly, the deacons exercised a range of tasks in this way but, if we follow the examples of Philip and of Paul and his companions, these included the establishing and founding of new communities through service and the ministry of the word.

The newly revised *Common Worship* ordination service for deacons embraces both of these understandings of what it means to be a deacon (in contrast to the earlier ordinals which emphasized only the 'servant' or 'apprentice priest' element).

As an example of the element based on loving service, the bishop says in the introduction to the service:

> Deacons are ordained so that the people of God may be better equipped to make Christ known. Theirs is a life of visible self-giving. Christ is the pattern of their calling and their commission; as he washed the feet of his disciples, so they must wash the feet of others.

As an example of the second, the charge to deacons contains the following:

> Deacons are called to work with the Bishop and the priests with whom they serve as heralds of Christ's kingdom. They are to proclaim the gospel in word and deed, as agents of God's

purposes of love. They are to serve the community in which they are set, bringing to the Church the needs and hopes of all the people. They are to work with their fellow members in searching out the poor and weak, the sick and lonely and those who are oppressed and powerless, reaching into the forgotten corners of the world, that the love of God may be made visible.[11]

According to Church of England liturgy, deacons are heralds of Christ's kingdom and agents of God's purposes of love. There is therefore, I want to argue, an appropriate match between the New Testament understanding of the term deacon and the role of the pioneer minister who seeks to establish a fresh expression of church. The pioneer minister acts not on their own behalf but in a recognized and representative capacity not only on behalf of a particular congregation but in a public way on behalf of the whole Church. They are an ambassador and appointed representative. The pioneer minister begins the establishing of a fresh expression through service and the formation of new communities, exactly the foundation of diaconal ministry. The pioneer minister enables the gospel to cross cultural boundaries through incarnational ministry: living among people, sharing their lives, seeking to see the gospel take root in a new culture. Humility is at the very heart of what it means to be a pioneer in this way. We do not take our own concepts of church with us but, as servants of the gospel and the new community, we seek to see church emerge following a shape dictated by the new culture. The pioneer minister, like Philip and Paul, seeks to proclaim the powerful, life-giving and life-shaping message of the gospel in appropriate ways within this new community in order to see a new Church brought into being.

For the working out of this model in practice, there is again no better place that the speech to the Ephesian elders in which Paul describes, the first part of the speech, this diaconal ministry in establishing a new congregation in Ephesus:

> You yourselves know how I lived among you the entire time from the first day that I set foot in Asia, serving the Lord (*diakoneo*) with all humility and with tears, enduring the trials that came through the plots of the Jews. I did not shrink from doing anything helpful, proclaiming the message to you and teaching you publicly and from house to house.
>
> (Acts 20.18-20)

Paul is here exercising a ministry which Luke calls 'deaconing', which embraces incarnational mission ('you know how I lived'), humility, the formation of new communities, proclamation and suffering for the sake of the gospel.

It is in *diakonia*, therefore, that we find the New Testament and theological underpinning for the calling of the pioneer minister, the first task of ministry identified in the opening paragraphs of this chapter. The calling is deeper and richer than the calling to be an evangelist – the call to live and proclaim the gospel in a variety of different contexts. This is a calling to serve, through service to form community, in community to sow the gospel and gather a new congregation.

Presbyters or priests:[12] sustainers of missionary communities through word and sacrament

At the heart of the ministry of Jesus is prayer for others, seen in the ministry of healing, and the ministry of teaching and preaching. This dual focus is connected and taken up by Luke in his representation of the ministry of the twelve in Acts 6.4:

> We will devote ourselves to prayer and the *diakonia* of the word.

The dual emphasis of the ministry of the word and the prayers is taken up elsewhere in the New Testament and forms the basis for presbyteral ministry. As the Church develops its theology of the sacraments, so word and sacrament together form the heart of the ministry of the priest. Sacramental ministry is in turn focussed on baptism (the admission of new members to the community with accompanying preparation and instruction) and presiding at the Eucharist (the meal that nurtures and sustains the community in its journey). The purpose of these ministries, as expounded in Ephesians 4 and elsewhere, is the sustaining and equipping the whole Church for ministry and mission.

Within the New Testament there is support for presbyteral ministry being raised up locally in response to the preaching of the word. This is clearly the pattern in Acts 13 and 20, passages which bracket the great period of missionary and church planting activity described in the central section of Acts. There is also support for those who exercise these ministries coming in from beyond the local congregation (as with Barnabas and Paul himself to Antioch and Apollos to Ephesus and Corinth).

I don't need to make the case here for the place of presbyteral or priestly ministry within established, traditional churches. This is already part of the way in which the Church of England operates across its thousands of parishes. It is also clear to me that as fresh expressions of church mature, the ministry needed will change. They are established by those whose ministries are primarily diaconal. They are sustained and nurtured in their teaching and sacramental life by those whose ministries are presbyteral or priestly. Throughout the history of Christian mission, as today, there have been those who establish a new community through pioneering gifts and whose ministry develops into one of sustaining that same community. There are other examples (not least Paul himself) of those called to pioneer new congregations over and over again.

As in the first centuries of the Church, so in the present missionary context, particular care needs to be taken in the making of disciples, the preparation of new Christians to receive the sacrament of baptism and to live out their baptism. This is as much at the heart of the priestly ministry as presiding at the Eucharist, and space must be created for this task within the life and ministry of the priest. As Rowan Williams argues in Chapter 4 above, the ordering of the new community around the Eucharist is, likewise, central to this calling.

A number of issues arise about the provision of presbyteral ministry within fresh expressions of church. Should the presbyters be found and raised up within the new communities as happens in Acts 13? Certainly there is a strong case for this. The wisdom of the worldwide Church and the missionary movement suggest that local leadership is vital for the flourishing of communities – as George Lings argues. However, the received Anglican pattern of presbyters being also normally called in from outside and of a cross-connection of ministries has both a long tradition here and clear New Testament roots. The different cultures within the United Kingdom are distinct but also part of one broader British culture.

Should the deacons who have called and established the community also become the presbyters who provide the sustaining and discipling ministry? Clearly this is happening in a number of instances in fresh expressions of church. It was also the case in the newly established Pauline churches that, where he could, Paul remained for two or three years (as in Corinth and Ephesus) in order to undertake this establishing ministry. However, it may also be the case, in some instances, that particular individuals are so gifted in pioneering diaconal ministries that they should be deployed by the wider Church to focus on this calling, with others alongside to sustain and nurture the new communities.

Finally, and necessarily briefly, should we abandon our historic patterns of ordained ministry altogether in order to provide the emerging new communities with a sacramental life through lay people presiding in baptism and at the Eucharist? To do so as a recognized norm would run counter to the wisdom that we inherit from the past: that the health and well being of the Church is best served through the ordination of particular people to these ministries of service and leadership within the community. The call to sustain and enable missionary communities, which is at the heart of the call to be a priest, cannot easily be separated from presiding at the Eucharist.

Exercising episcope: enabling others and connecting the Church together

The Greek word *episcope* simply means watching over. It carries an active rather than a passive meaning. In the Septuagint, the Greek Old Testament, the word also carries the meaning to visit. We should have in mind therefore a proactive, protective, missional watching over not the role of a passive spectator.

The qualities and ministries of those called to exercise *episcope* centre on four roles, identified in the New Testament and developed in the Christian tradition:[13]

Watching over yourself
Those exercising this ministry need the maturity and discipline to oversee their own lives and development as well as the ministry of others. The foundation for this understanding is present in Acts 20.28 ('Keep watch over yourselves and over the all the flock') and re-inforced by Gregory the Great's Pastoral Rule and Richard Baxter's classical text, *The Reformed Pastor*.

Enabling others in ministry
Historically, bishops have had a role in calling, equipping and sending others in different forms of ministry. Those who exercise *episcope* today have a similar role and calling.

Guarding, guiding and building missionary communities
In this, the role of episcope overlaps with that of presbyter except that the person exercising episcope will normally be charged with the care of a number of congregations.

Location, representation and connection
The person exercising episcope establishes and holds the relationships between different communities. He, or she, is the public representative of these congregations to the wider society.

Recent Anglican documents on the ministry of the bishop (including *Mission-shaped Church*), have emphasized the pro-active and missionary nature of the leadership the bishop is called to exercise. *Episcope* is not to be simply a stewardship of existing resources and congregations but a dynamic seeking of new opportunities for mission and the establishing of new communities.

Where is *episcope* needed within the mixed economy Church? Clearly the ministry of bishops is vital within dioceses, co-ordinating the ministry and mission of the whole people of God within a larger area. However, and equally clearly, there is a need for episcope to be exercised at a much more local level at the level of the deanery, groups of churches and larger parishes, particularly (but not exclusively) by those called to be stipendiary ministers.

Three dimensions in a mixed economy

We therefore have in our inherited Anglican tradition of ministry a biblical and helpful set of concepts for ministry in a mixed economy Church. At the heart of the life of each parish will be a person or group of people exercising *episcope*. This person or group will have oversight of a number of stable communities of Christians, both traditional churches and maturing fresh expressions of church all of which will need the ministry of presbyters. The task of the presbyters is to sustain these communities through the ministry of word and sacrament, paying particular attention to the call to make disciples and to form missionary community. The person or group will also exercise *episcope* over a number of different fresh expressions of church established and begun by those who are exercising diaconal ministries: forming community through service and sowing the seed of the gospel. The normal 'shape' for parish ministry will therefore look something like the diagram overleaf.

The picture will be continually changing as some fresh expressions mature into established congregations and as others are started or do not mature and continue.

'Lay' and 'ordained' ministries

I would argue that most aspects of all of these dimensions of ministry can and should be exercised by lay people as well as those who are ordained to the traditional roles. *Episcope* in almost every context should be exercised collaboratively as a shared ministry of those who are ordained and those who are lay. There are certainly contexts in which lay people alone might exercise

87

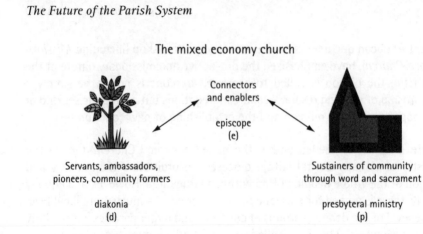

The mixed economy church

Connectors
and enablers

episcope
(e)

Servants, ambassadors,
pioneers, community formers

Sustainers of community
through word and sacrament

diakonia
(d)

presbyteral ministry
(p)

And like this in a more developed form:

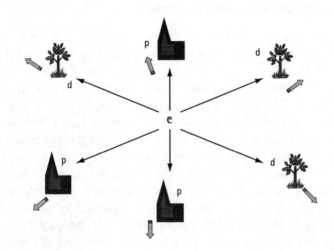

or focus on this role. A recognized lay minister who presides over a network of cells in a local church would be one example. An example of shared episcope might be a leadership team working across a multi-parish benefice seeking to see the establishing of fresh expressions alongside existing congregations.

Recognized lay ministers already exercise aspects of presbyteral ministry in the ministry of the Word and the leading of worship, the central calling of Reader ministry and, informally, as catechists, leaders of children's groups, facilitators of discipleship courses and in other ways.

Lay ministers exercise *diakonia* in a representative way as pioneers as licensed evangelists within the Church Army or recognized through a diocesan licence or parochial recognition.

If lay as well as the ordained are able to exercise these ministries then what is the point and distinctive of ordination as a bishop, priest or deacon? Ordained ministry continues to bear witness to two vital factors in the Christian tradition of ministry.

The first is that ministry in the way of Jesus Christ is about the whole person, not simply a task or role. Although all may exercise any particular task as part of their ministry (apart from the particular rites of presiding at the Eucharist, pronouncing absolution, baptism, confirmation and ordination), those who are ordained are seeking in a deeper way the integration of their life, character and calling with the exercise of these ministries in and on behalf of the whole Church.

The second and related factor is the lifelong nature of these callings, in and on behalf of the Church, which allows for growth in wisdom and character. It is one thing to be called to exercise pioneer ministry for five or six years in one's early twenties before embarking on a different career (also in response to God's call). It is another to seek ordination as a lifelong commitment to the deaconate or the priesthood.

We need ordained bishops, priests and deacons to affirm this lifelong calling, recognized by the churches, and the integration over time of the person with the office: the accumulation of wisdom in pastoral care and mission. We need recognized lay ministries in all of these areas in order to create space and give authority to those whose callings may change and develop at different times of their life and whose sphere of Christian service may be beyond as well as on behalf of the churches.

Stipendiary and self-supporting ministries

From the time of the New Testament onwards there have been recognized Christian ministers, who have been self-supporting, and those who have been supported through the gifts and generosity of others mediated through the Church.

The last 50 years have seen a massive recovery in the valuing of recognized self-supporting ministry in the Church of England in a range of ways such that there are now many more self-supporting lay and ordained ministers than stipendiary ministers.

It is clear that for theological, practical and pastoral reasons, self-supporting ministry will need to be nurtured and encouraged in all three dimensions of ministry in the mixed economy Church. However, I would make a particular case for restoring models of self-supporting ministry in the exercise of *diakonia* and pioneering ministry. This is appropriate and wise from the perspective of sustainability: we simply cannot afford a large number of stipendiary posts to begin new initiatives (although I believe we need to create some in every diocese).

It is vital also to avoid creating pastoral dependence on paid clergy who are expected to do everything in small new communities. This is a highly significant lesson learned from the world mission and church planting movements. It also matches well Paul's model of diaconal ministry: serving in order to create community creates an obligation not to be a burden to those one is serving (Acts 20.32-34).

Conclusion

As the Church adjusts to a post-Christendom situation, the demands of ministry become more complex. It is tempting to look for our new models either outside our tradition altogether or by attempting (mistakenly) to recover a 'more primitive' charismatic tradition which we imagine lies beneath the emerging New Testament picture.

However, there is immense potential, flexibility and wisdom in the threefold patterning of ministry that we inherit from the New Testament tradition and the history of the churches: a pattern that can shed light on and help shape lay as well as ordained ministries in the Church today.

We continue to need (and God continues to call) recognized lay and ordained ministers to sustain and enable stable missionary communities: traditional churches and maturing fresh expressions of church.

We continue to need (and God continues to call) those who can share in the collaborative oversight of parishes, deaneries and dioceses through the ministry of *episcope*: not simply a passive care of what already is but an active imagining and bringing to birth of new communities in mission.

We are rediscovering our need (and God is beginning to call) men and women who will exercise diaconal ministry in recognized ways on behalf of congregations. A threefold ministry is needed in developing a mixed economy Church.

PART THREE:
WAYS FORWARD

7

Doing traditional church really well

Robin Gamble

If we are to develop a mixed economy of churches, this will mean continuing to enable every traditional parish church to flourish, to be mission-shaped and to grow. Robin Gamble brings passion, wisdom and enormous experience to his subject. He is currently Canon Missioner in Manchester Diocese and was previously Adviser in Evangelism in the Diocese of Bradford and Vicar of St Augustine's in the city. He has helped pioneer many new initiatives in church life and evangelism and, with others, shares in leading the influential courses, 'Leading your church into growth'.

It *is* still there, scattered throughout the length and breadth of a multi-faith post-Christendom England. In the villages; the suburbs; the housing estates (both the posh and the poor ones); it's still in the inner city and the city centre; it's in the market towns and the new towns. The pubs and the post offices might be disappearing but despite all these years of decline the parish church keeps on hanging on.

'Inherited' and 'emerging' belong together, overlapping, interweaving and mutually supporting. In this loving relationship, traditional church is not in fading away mode; she is both older sister and parent to the newly born. As such she needs to be a generous sister/parent, sharing experience, wisdom and resources while also being open to receive back freshness and youthful vigour. On a recent visit to the West Country I discovered a beautiful example of this relationship in action. The well-attended and healthy parish church was advertising 'WOW' (Worship on Wednesday). This was not just a new time but also a new type of church. Interestingly, the friends we were staying with, who sit rather on the edge of 'traditional church', were clearly positive and interested in 'WOW'.

The traditional parish church

It is possible to produce a list of common features that form the skeleton of the English parish church.

A large, prominent building, that is usually one of the most interesting, attractive and valued, in the local neighbourhood. Unfortunately it is also likely to be one of the most demanding and expensive to maintain.

A vicar (male or female), who is instantly recognizable in that role, when wearing a dog collar. In most cases, the vicar is trusted and wanted. Doors of all types are open to them. The unchurched and the de-churched are equally happy to discuss life, God and the universe with 'the vicar'!

Even in these days of multi-parish benefices where there are many parishes (usually with small populations) without their own individual vicar, the overall picture remains of a well-staffed national Church. Meanwhile, the ever increasing dimension of OLMs, NSMs, youth and community workers, evangelists and administrators, all bring lots of new possibilities to the table.

A congregation, consisting of 'locals' and of those who travel in but still harbour a real warmth for church and parish. The congregation may have lots of things 'missing' but, despite appearances, it will also contain an amazing quality of commitment, goodwill and generosity. It will often be the largest community group in the area.

A parish, which, alongside the human networks of all congregational members, creates a dual sort of mission field. We may look upon this dual mission field as a meaningless lump of several thousand indifferent people. Research, however, shows that a considerable number of them greatly value and feel close to 'their' church.

A weekly service, which, in many cases, may be a rather neglected, 'not quite sure what it is anymore' event. For many, it is a 'grey' and boring experience. There are signs however that we are beginning to make it something of depth, life, colour and

relevance that actually touches and draws people in. Over a
million adults attend these services every week.

Beyond this we could go on to talk about:

- the still massive, ministry of occasional offices;
- our considerable range of community activities;
- a huge presence in schools and colleges;
- the annual cycle of festivals, which brings so many people to our doors;
- a world of children's activities for which we provide volunteers and premises;
- the continuing interest shown in us by local and national media;
- the extensive networks, support and shared experience that exists at deanery, diocesan and national Church levels;
- the generous giving that exists in most churches and the still solid economic base.

Last, but certainly not least, we could say something about the amazing level of trust which society at large places in us. We are seen as 'safe', approachable and good. The vast majority of people who don't attend their parish church have still got some sort of remembered affection for it. In what Grace Davie calls 'vicarious religion' (see Chapter 3 above) they are glad that we are there, and many of them will call on us at some stage in their life.

Frankly, it is too easy to be gloomy and dismissive about inherited church. We can read the above list with a negative, half-defeated mindset or with a sense of hope in our hearts that feels much more positive and laden with potential. If we were to offer this assembly of pieces, to a new religious group trying to get off the ground, or to an emerging political party wanting to launch themselves nationally, they would bite our hand off and beam with optimism and excitement.

So, given that we have this huge infrastructure, mighty group of people and general sense of goodwill towards us, what does it mean to 'do traditional church well'?

Doing things really well

The vision, surely, is about being a healthy and growing Church. As with all organic life forms such as a vine, flock or body, well-being, health and growth all work together because 'All living things grow'.

Over the last 25 years 'the parish church' has seen tremendous qualitative growth in almost every part of its life – spirituality has deepened; community involvement has grown; liturgy has developed; giving has become more generous; ministry has flowered. The one aspect where it has not grown is quantity. The numbers of people coming to faith, being confirmed, and taking part in our life of worship have continued to decline.

Overall it is an encouraging picture. The 'parish church' is doing well and has seen considerable growth in recent years, but, and it's a big but, there is still one part of our life where we are not 'doing it well'. Our proclaiming of the gospel and inviting of men and women to follow Jesus and 'join with us' is still defective. In this one key area we are not 'well and healthy', we are diseased.

So if we want to 'do it well' we need to continue developing what is healthy while remedying what is unwell.

A personal journey of discovery

In 1995 I became the 'Evangelism Adviser' in the Diocese of Bradford. Soon I was leading missions, speaking at evangelistic events and helping to set up enquirers groups. This all felt very worthwhile with people becoming Christians, going deeper in their spiritualities, and coming closer into church life.

After a while, however, I began to wonder. There was *activity and action*, but much of it felt a bit like a 'bolt on extra' to church life. Increasingly, I sensed a need to go one step further back. I began spending time with churches looking at their overall strategy. Together we started thinking about long-term goals and objectives; the use of resources, time and energy; the quality of worship and church family life. We were into the realm of prioritization, *vision and planning*. This seemed to be more demanding, but ultimately more life changing and productive.

Then I had another bout of wondering. It seemed to me that there was yet another step, one stage further back. Eventually, I found myself asking churches, clergy and lay leaders to think about their *basic hunger or desire*. What did they really want to see happen in their church and ministry? Did they want to see their church just keep going week by week? Were they content to see a few new faces from time to time? Or did they have a more profound desire? Did they share the passionate hunger and desire of a missionary God?

This was my personal journey. It began with action then moved backwards to planning and eventually led right back to desire. I discovered that both I, as an evangelist, and the local church (if it wanted to 'do the job well') needed to reverse the process. The starting point is desire, which then finds a meaningful shape through planning, and finally emerges into appropriate and productive action. The story of Nehemiah is a picture of the outworking of desire, plan and action. When he first learns of the true state of Jerusalem in ruins, he is weepingly heart broken. An honest assessment, passion and desire are all involved. He then moves on to draw up a strategic plan and put it into action. The energy which derives from his passionate desire keeps him close to God and enables him to overcome the obstacles. Surely this is the way God's own mission operates, having its genesis in his heart and its field of action in the world of needy human beings.

The key to doing 'inherited church well' is to be a 'well church' and well-being is about healthy DNA. It seems to me now that the DNA for a healthy growing church is:

The next key questions are how do we do 'Desire, Plan, Action' and what do they look like in the context of a conventional parish church?

Passionate desire

Desire is not just a human egotistical pursuit of desire for success. Rather it is something growing out of the very heart of God himself. It is prompted by the Holy Spirit and is at the same time the place in our inner self where we actually receive his empowering. Jesus spoke to the hungry and desiring disciples when he said 'you will receive power when the Holy Spirit has come upon you' (Acts 2.8). This manner of spiritual desire is closely linked to, and by, prayer.

In preparation for this chapter I went to see my friend, Adrian, an

Anglo-Catholic priest. He has been vicar of his East Manchester working-class parish for three years. The church is growing steadily, in numbers, and depth. I asked for the three key factors that led to this growth. Factors two and three took a bit of thinking about – they eventually emerged as powerful worship and good biblical teaching. Factor number one, however, shot straight out. More than anything else, he puts it all down to prayer. Adrian prays a lot. He also teaches his people to pray, in their private lives and in their meetings and services. Like Nehemiah, Adrian faces a massive rebuilding job and, like Nehemiah, he is hurt by the status quo of decline. The hurt and desire turned him to pray.

Spiritual desire does three things for a church – it shapes the mission; energizes the mission and overcomes the mission negatives.

Shaping the mission

There are numerous ideas, projects and strategies all demanding of time, energy and resources. We are constantly tempted to do too much, have too many initiatives, spread ourselves too thin and get lost in a world of half-finished schemes. Desire moves us away from the lots of quite good ideas to the few God ideas. It gives us back our Jesus mission shape. It helps us to prioritize and forces us to make difficult decisions.

Some time ago I met a parish priest who was two years away from retirement. He wanted my advice on what he should focus on for this final spell of time. Based in a close community with a tremendous ministry of pastoral, loving presence, everyone knew and valued him. I suggested he could spend most of his final two years visiting some of those who had valued his ministry, and inviting them to join a Christian enquirers group. He was also, however, vicar of a beautiful church building, a part of which was in need of restoration. In making his decision to use the time and energy of his last two years to raise money for restoration, his mission was shaped by his desire, but what sort of desire was it?

A huge area of decision making, which has threatened to almost tear the Church in two, is the choice between social, community gospel work and evangelistic gospel outreach. Gordon Dey is vicar of a huge post-war Bradford council estate. For the last 20 years Gordon, working with a dedicated congregation, has built up the most effective mission of community care that I have ever seen. Some years ago, however, they took a major decision. They decided that alongside caring for the community they also wanted to share the Good News with the local people. The central desire at the heart of the church is of an expanding congregation of people, living the Jesus way, having an expanding influence on the whole estate. The shaping of their ministry reflects the desire in their hearts.

Empowering the mission

Jesus was a driven man. His desire to share God's love and change lives drove him on. The desire provided the drive, the energy and the motivation. His was a long, mission journey, a marathon, so he needed a lot of energy. Many clergy complain that they have got the desire, but their church hasn't, so for a church needing desire here are three places to revisit.

First, revisit the truth of your own situation. Take a good look at your growth or decline figures over recent years. Examine your attendance and confirmation statistics, your youth and children's work. Find out what's happening around major festivals, social events and community projects, put the results into graphs and see where they lead. Then present the hard truth to the PCC and congregation. The truth may encourage you to keep going on your chosen path or it may disturb you into a new kind of desire.

The second place to revisit in this building of desire process is the Bible. The Gospels and the Acts of the Apostles are the best books ever written about mission, church growth and evangelism. They have the power not only to instruct but also to inspire. When they are preached, taught, read and discussed by a church they massively increase desire.

The Eucharist is the third on my places to visit list. Too often we have allowed it to become a routine, predictable and safe ritual, lacking imagination, passion and a sense of the contemporary. For many it has slipped into being a mild and comforting help to their individual lives. In fact it is the sustaining and empowering missionary meal for the missionary Church. We need to revisit, rediscover and rebuild this weekly Eucharist. It is here that Jesus feeds us with his living body and blood, gives us his desire and motivation so that we can pray, 'Send us out in the power of your Spirit, to live and work to your praise and glory.'

Ultimately the Holy Spirit is the source of real mission empowerment. The Spirit is both the true source of spiritual desire and the response to that desire once it has been engendered. Taking a long truthful look at ourselves, opening the word and eating of the Eucharist are all key access points.

Overcoming mission negatives

In 2005 I met with a group of parish clergy. They were all involved in inherited mode Church, but were doing it in a missionary way. I asked them what were the obstacles facing their churches. They produced a list which included inappropriate Anglican liturgy, difficult buildings, exhausted leaders, apathetic and unwelcoming congregations, shortage of resources and unfruitful evangelistic projects. (This would actually make a good course of Bible studies.)

These are real but overcomable obstacles, but the overcoming needs hungry desire to provide the motivation. Churches that 'want it' overcome most of the barriers; those with low levels of desire often give up at the first fence. Desire makes us both more determined in ourselves and more dependent on our God.

Strategic planning

Manchester Diocese has got a major problem of long-term numerical decline, which in the late 1990s was registering 3.5 per cent a year. In this situation, we can either accept the decline and make plans to limit the damage, or we can do the exact opposite and find a way forward to be healthy and growing. We are taking the latter option and have built a whole strategy around our desire and need to grow, at the heart of which is a project called 'Plan for Growth'.

In 'Plan for Growth' we encourage each local church carefully and prayerfully to draw up a three-year development plan. This begins with them listing the various elements of church life and doing a simple health check. They then pick out three or four issues from the list and ask these questions.

- Where are we now?
- Where do we want to be in three years?
- How do we get there?

The 'Where are we now?' question is not just an internal, 'looking at our present state' examination, it is also about place, local culture, and mission context. Is yours a middle-class suburban situation or a working class outer estate one? Are you in a predominately white area, or are you a multi-cultural place? Are you in the south or the north, the town or the countryside? Is your context full of young people, families or the elderly? Mission context is not just about neighbourhood and parish, it is also about all the human networks in which our church members live their daily lives.

Thinking about your context will influence both your planning for healthy church and the sort of activities you set up. It will impact on the style, content, feel and even the timing of your worship. It will affect the type of preaching and teaching that you offer. The great Anglican tradition is that we are the Church of the people, that we are there belonging to and arising out of every neighbourhood and network culture. This vocation to incarnation should have a 'moulding influence' on every part of church life if we are to 'do the job well'.

Thinking about mission context should also inform judgements concerning fruitfulness or effectiveness. Clearly a job 'well done' in the post industrial north will look quite different from one in the London commuter belt, but it will be an equally valuable part of the whole.

A further aspect of the 'Where are we now?' question concerns the issue of single or multi parish benefices. Generally speaking, the basic issues of desire, planning and fruitful action, apply equally to both situations, but probably need a bit more thinking about where there is more than one church. The questions to consider are usually, 'Should this strategy be applied to all the churches in the group, at the same time or one at a time?' and 'Is it appropriate and helpful to think of one of the churches as a mother or minster church, setting the lead and supporting the others?'

In answering these questions the local churches effectively draw up their own individual road map or 'Plan for Growth'. Jesus had a road map for his mission from simple beginnings in Galilee to the climax in Jerusalem, preaching the kingdom and picking up followers on the way. Similarly, the Early Church had a plan, starting in Jerusalem, travelling through Judea and out into the Mediterranean. Here in Manchester we recognize that if we fail to plan then we are in effect planning to fail. We are 'Nehemiah-like' in our discomfort of long-term decline and so we are 'Planning for Growth'. The growth is broad-based, including all areas of church life but we make it clear that numerical growth is a good and vital part of the plan.

Roger Cooper is vicar of a healthy and growing church in Blackrod. They see themselves as Modern, Liberal Catholics. Roger describes them as a church with lots of ideas and fleeting thoughts and says that 'Plan for Growth' pinned them down and made them think through what they were really about, it focused their energy and desire. In contrast St Martin, Droylsden was a declining church in a difficult part of East Manchester. As a new vicar Donna Williams introduced 'Plan for Growth' to her PCC. It gave a sense of vision and direction and was 'a wake up call' for the church. It has encouraged more church members to get involved in ministry, and has encouraged the growth of the congregation from the low twenties to the high thirties. For them Plan for Growth was born in and has continued to be sustained by prayer.

Having a plan or strategy is a bit alien to most of us involved with Inherited Mode Church. Our natural language is that of presence, caring and weekly routine. We tend to be more into 'being' than planning. If we do plan then it is usually for the week ahead, or for the next festival rather than for a long-term vision. We are brilliant at being reactive to the 'what is', we are less good at being proactive and building the 'what can be'. None of these values need be threatened by the idea of longer-term planning. In fact they can be enhanced. If we take the Scripture stories seriously, we have to conclude that God is a long-term planner, being concerned for people in the here and now while also looking to build a better future for them.

Presence, proclamation, persuasion

Whenever I'm involved helping a church to build a planned way forward into health and growth, there is one piece of strategy that I always point to. It is called the 'three Ps' or Presence, Proclamation and Persuasion. Actually, the most successful churches turn it into the 'four Ps', by adding prayer. The 'Three Ps' strategy can be seen at various points in Paul's missionary work, but most clearly in the Ephesus story of Acts 19. Here Paul first establishes relationships through his presence in the market place, secondly he proclaims the Good News in the lecture hall and finally he spends quality time with those who want to know more by the work of gentle persuasion. Similarly, in the mission work of Jesus we can seem him establishing presence with acts of healing, then proclaiming the message and finally spending time with individuals. We can also see his preceding this threefold strategy with days and nights of prayer.

Presence

We are continually being told that the Church has lost its fringe, or has little traditional presence or is distant and remote. Two pieces of research I have been conducting seem to refute this line of thought.

In recent years I have worked with over 500 clergy in an exercise which asks them to estimate the number of people on the edge of or completely outside the church with whom they have had good pastoral contact over a typical two-month period. The average number is 24. In other words, in a typical year, a typical Anglican parish priest is involved in 144 'presence ministries'. In most cases the same typical priest is too busy, or too unaware, or too unplanned to follow up these beginnings. Paul and Jesus followed presence with proclamation, but our practice is to follow presence with more presence.

In a second exercise I work with local church leadership groups. I ask them to list their organizations, school involvements, community projects etc. To this they add their occasional offices, clergy contacts and congregational networks. Finally, they estimate and add up the numbers of people involved. The final figure is usually in the hundreds. This exercise shatters their 'Johnny no mates mentality' and opens up a whole new mission field including both the de-churched and the unchurched.

Taken together these exercises demonstrate something real and often neglected. Furthermore, if they are thought about in the context of Grace Davie's work, they show us that the traditional Church has a large and warmly interested mission field on the doorstep.

I have a vivid memory of a particularly strong and capable liberal parish priest in Sheffield. He had attended a 'Leading Your Church into Growth' training course, and realized that every time he launched an effective piece of community work he opened up a doorway into the faith for the recipients, but rather than completing the piece of work by helping some of these folk through the doorway, he rushed on to set up the next presence project.

Proclamation

In today's insecure Church we are wary of the word proclamation. It seems a bit aggressive, overly confident or exclusive in a multi-cultural context. Following the model of Jesus, the Early Church was a proclaiming missionary movement. For them, as for him, proclamation was seen as a kind and loving act; it was a sharing of Good News, an offering of invitations to a wonderful new life. It was an essential part of the kingdom experience. More than just words, it was an experience, often accompanied by healings, feasting and a general feel-good factor.

To hear the gospel message communicated in a passionate and contemporary way, and to experience this in a welcoming and enjoyable atmosphere can be a life-changing event. It should be seen as a basic human right. Sadly, I suspect, that most people, even most of those who enjoy our presence, never get to experience this sort of Christian proclamation.

Proclamation is far more do-able than most of us imagine. It can happen at festivals, occasional offices, community and school events – in church or at the pub, in a restaurant or local art gallery, out on the streets or in someone's home. There are now masses of good people and resources around to help the local church develop this work.

Kettlewell is a typical and beautiful dales village. Parish church does very well in the dales and in one sense doesn't need to worry too much about proclamation. In the case of Kettlewell, however, the local church had a strong desire to share the Good News. Every year the village holds an 'Epiphany Supper' which is usually more supper than epiphany. The church developed it as an opportunity to share the Epiphany Good News while still retaining all the traditional feel-good factor of the occasion.

Thorpe Edge is the exact opposite of Kettlewell. The tiny struggling council estate congregation decided that they wanted to invite the whole estate to church at Easter. Special services were planned, help and resources were brought in, prayer was deep and urgent, food and hospitality were good and warm. Lo and behold numbers of people came, and there was a strong response to the proclaiming of the Good News.

If we are to follow the Jesus pattern, the proclamation will always climax in invitation. An invitation to take one more step, to think more, talk more, pray more. As with Paul in Athens, the majority response to the proclamation is usually negative. Indifference, rejection and immersion in self-centred materialistic lifestyles accounts for most hearers. In every gathering, however, there are always the few who are searching, interested and wanting more. It is within this understanding of the 'significant few' that persuasion is most important.

Persuasion

Persuasion is not spiritual 'arm twisting'. Rather it is sensitive, listening and sharing, helping searchers towards the threshold. It is just this sort of helpful and patient ministry that Paul moves into with a few individuals after his great 'proclamation' at the Areopagus in Athens. We see a similar pattern when Jesus moves from the crowded market square of Jericho to spend personal time with Zacchaeus in his own home.

Persuasion can be one to one; it can be a small group experience. Much has been done in recent years about Christian enquirers groups. They are valuable, not just as proclamation 'follow-ons', but as stand-alone projects in their own right.

Some churches have developed their own course for an enquirers' group but most use prepared materials. The two most popular courses for Anglicans are *Emmaus*, which is seen as having a broad church appeal and *Alpha*, with the major advantage of being promoted through a national advertising campaign every Autumn. 'Start!' is the new 'kid on the block' by CPAS, a six-week course that begins where people really are.

Running an effective group is a three-step process. Step one is the contacting and inviting of people. Running an enjoyable, and effective exploring course is the second step. The third, and often neglected, movement is about helping people to carry on from the course into a committed pattern of discipleship, spirituality and church membership.

The classic pattern for Presence, Proclamation and Persuasion is to begin with a large number of people which reduces through self selection at each stage, resulting in a few coming through to commitment and spiritual maturity. This was the pattern both for Jesus and Paul. In effect it is the Parable of the Sower, with the few at the end producing real and lasting fruit.

Planning to do parish church well

Each church needs its own tailor-made plan. Though every plan will be different there are certain common building blocks that will probably feature in most cases. Space does not allow us to go into detail, but here is a simple list:

- creating a collaborative leadership team with shared vision;
- encouraging deep and continuing prayer;
- implementing the Presence, Proclamation, Persuasion strategy;
- establishing a sound financial base and resolving any building issues;
- making sure that weekly worship is alive, attractive and user-friendly both to committed members and new-comers;
- building a family atmosphere, with warm welcome, real relationships and pastoral care;
- deepening the spirituality of core members.

The most important issue on the list is, of course, worship. Today we operate in what Grace Davie calls a 'culture of choice'; rather than the past one of 'obligation'. So there is a need to re-model our church services making them warm and welcoming, relevant and meaningful. We can preserve and revitalize the best of the past alongside the contemporary. Language, imagery, music and the length and feel of our liturgy has to be carefully worked at to produce something that people will choose to be part of.

Working to a long term plan means:

- Don't do everything quickly, pace yourself.
- Stick to the plan, be focused and disciplined.
- Tweak and adapt the plan as you progress.
- Get help, from other churches, diocesan officers or a parish consultant

Action that works

There is no shortage of action in the average parish church; in fact there is usually too much of it. Every activity that we launch demands time, energy and resources – the three things that we feel short of. We are short of them because we squander them in too much diverse and unfocused action. The result is work that ends up being rushed and sometimes half-finished and a church left feeling too busy, tired out and resource starved. Then we wonder why it doesn't work. Jesus looked at people, trees and kingdom action and expected them to bear fruit. Effort, prayer and generous giving are not enough in themselves. They are supposed to be fruitful, that is, they are meant 'to work'. The answer is usually not to do more, but to do less and to do better

A piece of fruitful activity could be any of the following: introducing an enquirers group; setting up a mission weekend; planning a flower festival; launching a schools and young families project; creating a senior citizens luncheon club; initiating a series of improvements to the liturgy; running a stewardship scheme or developing small groups. Every piece of action that we launch should be part of our overall plan, not additional to it. There are two keys to fruit bearing action.

- *Carefully pray and prepare.* As any decorator will tell you, careful preparation leads to a 'quality job'. Work out exactly what you plan to do, how long it will take to set up and what resources will it need. What sort of follow up will be needed and what help and training will the team need? Make sure that the project you have in mind really does grow out of your long-term plan, rather than being a bolt-on extra.

  St John's church in Manchester have a three-year development plan that involves running enquirers' groups two or three times a year. Rather than waiting for a few enquirers to appear, they look ahead to suitable confirmation dates and then patiently work backwards allowing plenty of time for group meetings. Finally, they build in space to do invitations before the groups actually begin. They proactively prepare, pray and then act.

- *Think people before projects.* Take a good look at all the individuals you are working with and then find the right activity, material and resources to suit them, don't have a bright idea and then squeeze your people into it. Middleton and Heywood is a deanery on the edge of Rochdale. I was due to spend a three-week spell there doing and teaching evangelism. At the preparation stage there were lots of good ideas for action, but when we looked at the 'people map' it became increasingly clear that there was a problem. The churches had hundreds of children but there were hardly any teenagers. It was as if a Pied Piper suddenly played his tune and led the children away when they were about 12 years old. It was obvious that what energy and finance was available had to go into working with teenagers. A period of careful, prayed-through preparation ensued which eventually led to the establishment of a very successful deanery Christian youth group.

Every church has got its own 'people map'. Older children, families on the edge of church life, people who used to attend, family and close friends of church members and clergy contacts are often the key groupings to sketch in. Putting 'people before projects' will ensure that your mission in action will have the two great hallmarks of Jesus' own mission. First, it will have a foundation of good personal relationships. Secondly, it will be in context, culturally tuned in, and it will be incarnational.

These two key principles of prayerful preparation and of putting people first are clearly demonstrated by the Mission Weekends Project first launched by Springboard. Before planning any activities the churches involved think about their congregations, their fringe attenders, organizations, community links and schools work. Finally, they sift through lots of good ideas before settling on the two or three that will actually bear fruit for them. Mission weekends and similar activities work best when they dovetail into the presence ministry of the local church.

Every mission weekend, evangelistic project or proclamation event should be followed by the right sort of enquirers group using material that will actually work for the people involved. Similarly, the enquirers group needs to be taken deeper into discipleship. One of the most effective discipleship courses I have come across was devised by a parish priest who simply divided up the Eucharist into all its constituent parts and led her group through those parts week by week.

The amazing thing about Mission in Action is that something positive happens almost every time you do it, even when it is not very good. Some time ago I led a 'mission service' in a church in a very poor area of Salford. Frankly, the service was dismal bordering on the funereal, the music was lack lustre, the church was three quarters empty and my preaching was tired and incoherent. About a couple of weeks later I bumped into a very bright and intelligent young woman, in her mid-twenties, who had been at the service. With real joy she told me how she had spent the last fortnight 'walking the way', and how different her life was.

There is a tendency to think of this type of ministry as evangelical. This of course is doubly misleading. First, because it mistakenly assumes that all evangelicals are actively engaged and secondly, because it negatively writes off everybody else. Participating in God's mission, opening the door of faith, doing parish church well are all standard kingdom works. Just like prayer, kindness and worship they are part of what we are all supposed to be doing all of the time.

Doing traditional parish church well

The parish church is actually in far better shape that we often imagine. Yes there is long-term numerical decline and the ageing process, both of which we need to face up to. It is still, however, a large and resource-rich system, and it is still there, everywhere. Recent years have seen huge steps forward in terms of shared ministry, community involvement, commitment to peace and justice, ecumenical and multi-faith relationships, children's work, stewardship and spirituality.

Essentially, the parish church is about a great world-loving God and his people – congregation and clergy, office-holders and PCCs, people in the core and those on the edge. Together we are a truly amazing bunch, full of love, commitment, experience and spirituality. There are more of us and there is more about us, than we realize. We have allowed ourselves to become a bit weary, and a bit low on confidence and self-esteem. It is about time we buried these negatives and saw ourselves as God sees us and as we truly are. We are the history changers, the beacon bearers, the compassionate ones, the people of the living word.

'Doing Church well' is not about running a neat and tidy parish church, it is rather about being the growing, healthy mission-shaped church that has its genesis in the very heart of God and then travels out into the world of God. If we are to be well, healthy and growing, then we need good DNA.

- Desire – hunger and passion to be the church that God wants;
- Plan – development, growth and goals all following God's path;
- Action – bearing the fruit that God longs to see.

Desire, Plan and Action is not a slick formula, or a recipe for instant success. It is rather a journey, a movement. It arises out of the biblical story and is attested to by the continuous saga of the Church being done well. It is a friend and a guide to all of us today who still long to see the Church as a living, thriving, organic reality in the world.

Discussion questions

On a scale of 1 to 10 how strong is your desire to see your church grow?

Do you have a long term development plan for your church?

What could be the single most effective piece of action that could help you grow?

Helpful books

Bob Jackson, *Hope for the Church*, Church House Publishing, 2002.

Robert Warren, *Building Missionary Congregations*, Church House Publishing, 1995.

Lawrence Singlehurst, *Sowing, Reaping, Keeping*, Crossway Books, 1995.

Other resources

A training course for clergy and lay leaders 'Leading Your Church into Growth' details available at www.leadingyourchurchintogrowth.org.uk

'Start!' – A Christian Enquirers course – CPAS

Copies of 'Plan for Growth' can be obtained from Manchester Diocesan Office on 0161 828 1400.

8

Good practice is not what it used to be: Accumulating wisdom in fresh expressions of church

Michael Moynagh

The Church of England is following a call to develop many fresh expressions of church alongside traditional churches. Michael Moynagh distils here some of the wisdom being gathered in a thousand or more different places. He writes of the urgent need to gather this wisdom and make it widely available across the churches. Michael is co-director of the Tomorrow Project and a core member of the Fresh Expressions team. He is the author of a number of books including emergingchurch.intro.

Good practice is high on the agenda of fresh expressions of church – new and different forms of Christian community designed to fit the cultures of people who currently don't attend church. Church leaders and others wanting to know more about fresh expressions are asking, 'What do they actually involve?' Many who are exploring innovative forms of church, and who are often hesitant and uncertain about what they are doing, are looking for help.

This chapter is in two parts. The first sets out a framework for thinking about how Godly wisdom in initiating fresh expressions can be acquired. It describes why this is important, suggests an approach and provides a theological rationale. The second part highlights some issues around good practice that are already emerging, and which we might understand better if we had a more systematic approach to accumulating wisdom in fresh expressions.

The terms 'wisdom' and 'good practice' are used interchangeably. The language and use of good practice in the secular world risk leaving the notion floating on a sea of technique – good practice is simply good method. Here 'good practice' is understood more theologically – roughly, as Godly good practice (hence its association with wisdom).

More precisely, wisdom in fresh expressions is understood as good practice that satisfies the following criteria:

- theologically informed;
- evidence that it works well – or good reason to think it might;
- reproducible principles that give room for the Spirit to move;
- recognized by 'experienced others' that it is good practice when described to them.

Applying wisdom in fresh expressions requires you to discern what pieces of recognized good practice will enable you to accomplish specific tasks, and how those experiences should be adapted to your circumstances.

Wisdom can be learnt

The importance of learning wisdom

There are a host of obvious reasons why being wise in undertaking new forms of church is important. Practical wisdom is highly prized in Scripture, for example; individuals can be hurt and God's reputation can suffer when experiments in being church go wrong; wisdom may allow emerging expressions of church to reach their full potential. The Book of Proverbs and other passages make it clear that wisdom can be learnt. In the context of fresh expressions, how should this learning occur?

The question needs some thought because it is not easy to go straight from the question, 'What is good practice?' to the answer, 'It is . . .' There are no text books or manuals of instruction, and even if there were they would be quickly out of date. You have to put in a middle question, 'How do we discover good practice?', before you can reach the answer.[1]

The need for this extra question is vital – for at least three reasons.

1. Knowledge is more dynamic than in the past. In our faster, faster world, good practice spreads across the globe ever more quickly. In the world of work, new techniques are rapidly communicated through trade journals, networks within multinational companies, conferences and business schools. Good practice in London may be given a new twist in Hong Kong, may be developed further in Los Angeles and return to London, where it is improved yet again.

So asking 'What is good practice?' raises the question, 'How do I know if the answer I've got today has not already been superseded somewhere else?' This is especially pertinent to fresh expressions. When so much experimentation is going on in Australia, Britain, New Zealand and the USA, how can we be sure that we are up to date with wisdom, as it evolves?

2. Knowledge is more dispersed. In the past a manager would know how the job should be done and train a recruit to do it. But as economies have climbed the skills ladder, jobs have become more sophisticated and specialized. What was once a single job may now be undertaken by two or three specialists. Often a new recruit, with specific expertise, will know more about how to do the job than the manager. Knowledge is spread around more people.

    That is clearly the case with fresh expressions. New expressions of church are not so similar that one person can have a model of good practice and pass it on. Rather, the extraordinary diversity of fresh expressions means that there are already dozens of experts working in a wide variety of contexts – for example, among children in inner cities, teenagers in suburbs, youth on outer estates and in schools in a county town. Dispersed knowledge forces the question, 'How can I discover the wisdom that exists in so many places?'

3. Knowledge is becoming more deliberative. As knowledge has become increasingly dispersed, organizations have discovered that new knowledge can often best be created through the deliberation of practitioners. Bringing people in the know together to debate and discuss what they do generates fresh insights. Urban Expressions, a network of practitioners exploring new forms of church in urban contexts, is beginning to do this, with positive results.

    So if it is no longer true that individuals alone create knowledge, but teams do, it is not enough to ask, 'What is good practice for fresh expressions?' We must also ask, 'What processes would generate new understandings of good practice?' Good processes for creating good practice are part of good practice itself.

Acquiring and developing knowledge of good practice

Helping practitioners, church leaders, researchers and others discover and develop wisdom in pioneering new forms of Christian community is a priority for Fresh Expressions, the team set up by the Archbishops of Canterbury and York and the Methodist Council to encourage new or different culturally appropriate forms of church within the Anglican and Methodist denominations and beyond.

Adapting an approach from the secular world,[2] the team has conceptualized the application of wisdom in the following way. A fresh expression might ask:

- What are our key objectives?
- What tasks would we need to perform well to achieve each objective?
- How might those tasks be undertaken? (i.e., 'what theologically informed knowledge do we need and how can we plan to make sure we have it?')
- What would enable individuals and teams involved to discover better ways of doing those tasks?

Fresh Expressions proposes to support practitioners and others as they address the fourth question, using a threefold approach – connect, collect and reflect.

> *Connect* refers to learning networks that link up practitioners and enable them to learn from each other. These 'communities of practice' are increasingly important in secular organizations, and have a potentially valuable role within the Church. Fresh Expressions is discovering how to encourage and facilitate learning networks among practitioners.
>
> Experience suggests that to be effective, learning networks need regular face-to-face meetings, the capacity for members to seek help from each other online, occasional outside input to stretch those involved, a mixture of the familiar and the unusual, a rhythm to the network's life, permission for different levels of involvement and an enthusiastic co-ordinator. Learning needs to be intentional.[3]
>
> *Collect* refers to on-line knowledge libraries of how to do specific tasks, what constitutes good practice and whom to turn to for more detail. Individuals can collect knowledge needed for a particular task.[4] Fresh Expressions is developing an on-line guide to pioneering new forms of church. The guide will identify key tasks that practitioners are faced with, suggest theological principles that might inform how these tasks are undertaken, give examples of different ways in which these tasks have been approached and, where possible, describe personal attributes and skills that may be required.

The guide will be initially available in skeletal form, so that practitioners will be able increasingly to shape it through their contributions. With contributors' consent, visitors to the site will be free to contact individuals whose stories have been used. They will be encouraged to dialogue with each other, perhaps giving rise to learning networks. Specialist sections – for example, youth church – will be added in response to demand.

It is intended that the guide will be used by practitioners, trainers, mentors/coaches/accompaniers, researchers and church leaders wishing to encourage innovative types of church, and that insights from the guide will spread through networks.

Reflect refers to a variety of tools that enable practitioners to be genuinely reflective.[5] How many church practitioners, for example, undertake an important task for the first time without pausing to ask, 'Is there someone who has done this well and who could offer me good advice?' How many get regular and systematic feedback on what they do from others in the team, and discuss that feedback with a mentor or coach? These kinds of approach can be effective means of personal development – of discipleship, dare one say?

The separate elements – connect, collect and reflect – have the potential to be highly effective when combined together and reinforcing each other.

Theological rationale

This approach to acquiring wisdom in fresh expressions can be understood theologically in a variety of ways. One might be to highlight the following:

Stewardship: Connect, collect and reflect is about helping individuals to access the practical wisdom that will enable them to fulfil the creation mandate to care for the world.

Submission: Through the Incarnation, God in Christ placed himself in a situation where he had to learn from human beings the practicalities of everyday life – from table manners to carpentry. This is a huge affirmation of practical knowledge. Has the Church given sufficient attention to the acquisition of such knowledge? Connect, collect and reflect invite individuals to submit to the wisdom of those who have already made the journey.

Surrender: To be willing to submit to the knowledge of others, individuals must surrender their self-sufficiency in knowledge ('I know how to do it'). A Good Friday–Easter dynamic is involved. Individuals have to allow their presumption ('we know enough') to die so that new knowledge can rise up within them.

Spirit-led: The Spirit who came at Pentecost is the same Spirit who inspired the artisans to decorate the tabernacle (Exodus 35.31ff.) and dispenses the practical gifts of service and leadership, for example (Romans 12.6ff.). Might connect, collect and reflect be a vehicle for the Spirit, who leads Christ's followers into truth, to lead them into practical truths?

Shared: God's gift of the Church is a gift of Christian communities to serve the world. Sharing – of joys, disappointments, resources and lives – should be at the heart of each community and part of the connection between different expressions of church. Something would be wrong if the sharing of wisdom was not involved too. The tools we are proposing are designed to assist this sharing of wisdom so that the body of Christ can better serve other people – 'all of us are better than any of us'. At its heart, this will involve a shift from seeing knowledge as personal property ('I know') to viewing it as something held in common ('common knowledge').[6]

Celebrated: At the end of history, the results of accumulated, practical wisdom will be celebrated within the kingdom. As the new Jerusalem descends from the sky, the kings of the earth and the nations of the world will bring their achievements into the city (Revelation 21.24, 26). The triumphs of civilization – of good practice – will in some way be incorporated into the new creation. In anticipation, should not the Church be celebrating the fruits of shared, practical wisdom today? Sharing knowledge can be fun. Morale often goes up and people say, 'Of course, this is it. Why aren't we always doing this?'

Good practice in fresh expressions

As we have seen, central to accumulating wisdom in fresh expressions will be learning how to discover and disseminate Godly good practice. Obviously, techniques for doing this will be transferable to existing church – an example of how emerging forms of church have the potential to contribute to inherited church, as well as to be supported by it.

Systematic learning about good practice will help practitioners better understand how to undertake key tasks in relation to fresh expressions. In the limited space available, I consider six of these tasks, all of which would benefit from accumulated wisdom.

Pioneers' personal formation

As I have emphasized, it will be vital for fresh expressions that good practice is understood first and foremost theologically. It is about personal and collective discipleship. Following the discussion above, it is about how individuals and Christian communities grow in stewardship, submission, surrender, sharing and celebration. Led by the Spirit, good practice can be seen as a spiritual discipline. It is an aspect of how ministers, their fellow ministers and their expressions of church grow in Christ-likeness.

At the heart of good practice, therefore, is the notion of spiritual formation. Pioneers begin to express spiritual virtues when they ask, for example: 'What don't I know?' 'How can I learn from others?' 'How can I pass on to others what I do know?' 'How can I invite my colleagues to help me to be more self-aware?' As pioneers seek answers to these and other questions, they model good practice to their colleagues and find practical ways of helping their emerging communities to become more kingdom-shaped.

Good practice as a spiritual discipline puts the search for means firmly in the context of ends. Means – of doing fresh expressions better – are not sought for their own good. Means don't become the end. Rather, the search for better means becomes part of living in the light of the end – of the coming kingdom. Means are painted in God's colours.

Where to start

Behind fresh expressions is the assumption that 'we'll come to you' (wherever you are) rather than relying on 'you come to us' (here in 'our' church). This means that fresh expressions can take root in a huge variety of contexts – in the work place, in a club, in a school, in sheltered accommodation and many others. The potential for 'network' expressions of church that jump parish boundaries, such as deanery youth congregations, is great.

These opportunities have led some people to suppose that fresh expressions are an alternative to parish-based ministry. But this is far from the case. In the twenty-first century, the local is not to be written off. People certainly travel more, but they are also staying put. A Gallup poll found that 14 per cent of people had moved home in 1952. Half a century later, just 10 per cent of households had shifted in the previous year.[7] The figures are not strictly comparable, but they certainly do not suggest that Britain is becoming a nation of house movers.

Amazingly, according to the RAC Foundation, the number of households relocating in Britain because of jobs halved between 1984 and 1994.[8] When both partners work, more couples are saying, 'Let's not move every time one of us changes jobs. We'll make a base here, and if our jobs alter we'll commute the extra distance.' 'Relocation, Relocation' is little more than a television programme.

Place matters to people. As individuals stay in an area, they slowly get to know their neighbours. Some become friends. Individuals may 'talk to the world' by email, but they also connect with people round about. Not all networks are divorced from geography, which creates opportunities for church in local communities.

However, these communities are fragmenting. Ethnic groups, for example, have enriched many areas and added to the diversity. The number of households in Britain has increased by almost a third over the past 30 years, creating a demand for new homes – and the demand is set to grow further.[9] New housing estates tend to attract people with similar lifestyles. Not infrequently, these lifestyles differ from others nearby, fracturing the locality.

Census data show that Britain has been dividing more sharply on a geographical basis. Divisions between old and young, settled and migrant, black and white or rich and poor are more sharply based on geography now than 10 or 20 years ago.[10] Quite often these divisions are within parish boundaries.

As localities fragment, parish churches will have opportunities to think in terms not of a single local community, as in the past, but of different communities – a pastiche of housing estates, ethnic groups, lifestyle communities and people of various ages. Residents may identify more strongly with their particular group than with the village, the town or the suburb. The parish church may have to become even more local than in the past. New forms of local will require new forms of local church.

Wisdom in fresh expressions will value the opportunities that exist locally and see the parish in new ways. PCCs won't start by asking, 'How can we get people from different parts of the area into our one congregation?' Their first question will be, 'What are the various cultures here? Are there particular groups that we can serve, perhaps adding spiritual value in the process – parents, for example, homeless people, children after school or a new housing estate? What would some of us have to do to draw alongside these groups and be welcomed by them?'

Once a church has become immersed in some of its surrounding fragments it can ask, 'Can we help these fragments to join together from time to time?' Valuing the parish could create excellent opportunities for connecting fresh expressions to inherited modes of Christian community, giving life to the 'mixed economy' Church.

Cultural exegesis

Cultural exegesis means thoroughly understanding the culture of the people you want to serve. It may seem obvious that to serve people you need to understand them, but all too often Christians rush into mission without getting under the skin of those they seek to reach. With the best of intentions, they come up with an idea – perhaps a Christian café – and then look around for people who will welcome it. It is the old 'come to us' mindset, but in a different guise. Instead of 'come to our church', it is 'come to our coffee shop', 'come to our drop in centre' or 'come to whatever else we have in mind'. The starting point is not the aspirations of other people, but the enthusiasms of – frequently – a handful of Christians.

Good practice in fresh expressions means taking time to listen to people you might serve – to learn about their hopes and wants, to get inside their spirituality and to look at the world with their gaze. Just as Jesus immersed himself in the culture of his day, so Christians must soak themselves in the cultures of our day if they are to love the people involved and serve them through an expression of church.

There are lots of good ways of listening such as parish audits, various forms of survey, holding the equivalent of 'focus groups', moving on to a housing estate, in order to be right among the residents, or simply being more attentive to neighbours and local contacts.

One approach might be to start with networkers – individuals who know lots of people and who often can bring them together. A parish group exploring the possibility of a fresh expression might invite networkers in their congregation (or perhaps in the wider community) to describe their friends – what they were 'into', their needs and aspirations, how they thought about spirituality and so on.

Perhaps after several meetings, a picture of two or three networks might emerge, and ideas for serving them could be explored. A key question for the planning group would be whether the church actually had the appropriate resources to serve these networks. Periods of prayer, listening to the networkers, brainstorming, talking round and round, and Bible study might gradually yield some answers.

At the end of the 'cultural exegesis', the group would be in touch with networkers who could take representatives of the church into their networks. This would be better than what sometimes happens: churches collect all sorts of information about the parish, but are still left wondering, 'How do we make contact with this particular group of people?'

But this will be only one approach. Others will be different according to circumstances. Practitioners will be greatly helped if they can have examples of these different approaches and reflect on them.

Building in reproduction

Reproduction is fundamental to the life of the Church. At the end of Matthew's Gospel, Jesus told his disciples to reproduce what he had done. He had made them disciples, and they were to do the same with 'all nations' (Matthew 28.19). One way of reading Luke–Acts is to see how the life of Jesus was reproduced in the life of the Early Church.

Throughout history Christians have sought to reproduce themselves by planting new churches. The apostles reproduced something of the community life they had experienced with Jesus. The Jerusalem church then reproduced itself throughout the Middle East and into Europe and Asia. St Paul planted not just one church, but many. The process continues on today's new housing estates, where the Body of Christ still reproduces itself by establishing new churches.

Good practice for fresh expressions will involve continuing this process of reproduction, but without reproducing clones. Just as parents do not naturally reproduce clones of themselves, so fresh expressions will reproduce Christian communities that have something of a family likeness and yet also express their own distinctive character.

One reason for the parlous state of the Church in the West is that once established, churches have found it very difficult to reproduce. They slip into maintenance mode and fail to 'do it again'. Very best practice for fresh expressions will be to start new expressions of church that reproduce themselves again and again – expressions of church that beget children, who give birth to their own children, who in turn produce offspring.

How best to do this in our cultural context is still not clear. An American couple with full-time jobs have a gift for leading people to faith. As individuals become Christians, they are encouraged to invite their friends into their homes and lead a discovery Bible study for people who don't attend church. The couple will be part of the group for two sessions and then withdraw, providing support for the new Christian in one-to-one meetings and in other background ways. If the gathering emerges into a home-based church, members will be encouraged to do the same thing in their homes.

This approach may not work in other contexts – fundamental to fresh expressions is not to copy what others do, but to learn from them and do what best fits your own situation. Perhaps the lesson from this American example is that the couple stumbled on their approach after initially leading the discovery Bible studies themselves. They found that the group gathered by a new Christian became dependent on them and didn't reproduce. It was only as they, the mature Christians, withdrew that the group gained enough confidence to repeat the process.

Might this raise questions about the role of ordained clergy in fresh expressions? Might reproduction be more likely in some cases if clergy did not lead the expressions themselves, but supported and facilitated even the newest of Christians to become spiritual catalysts among their friends? What would be the implications for celebrating the sacraments? Answers to these questions will only emerge as practitioners experiment with a variety of approaches. It will be vital to have systematic ways of learning from these experiments.

Turning community groups into faith groups

If church is to connect with that growing segment of British society that has virtually no church background, fresh expressions may need to start not with a worship service, but with loving service.

If you start with Christian worship, it will be Christians who come! But if you first seek to respond to the perceived needs and aspirations of people with hardly any church experience, you will demonstrate genuine Christian love (which will be worth while in itself), and you may also draw them into a fuller and fuller expression of church that will enrich their lives. This raises the question: 'How can we move from loving service into a more rounded expression of church?'

Some fresh expressions of church start with an explicitly Christian element from day one. Service and proclamation join up straight away. Although it was not labelled 'church', a children's club in Milton Keynes attracted over 100 primary school children on a Saturday morning. The great majority were strangers to church. They started with board games and a variety of activities. Then there were warm-up activities for the whole group. Finally, there was a half-hour Bible story with application.

Parents knew in advance what the programme was. Some said, 'We're not into religion, but it probably won't harm the kids.' Often the sub-text was, 'Thank you for taking the children off our hands on a Saturday morning.' Many of the children, it seems, were just as grateful that the parents had been taken off their hands.

Other churches have run luncheon clubs and the like, with times of quiet 'spiritual' reflection at the end – perhaps some lighted candles, Christian music, a reading from Scripture, a few said prayers and an oasis of silence. Other café churches have met on Sundays, with coffee and newspapers available in one area, and testimony, a video presentation and a couple of Christian presentation songs in another. Community forms around the coffee, and individuals can duck in and out of the explicitly Christian dimension as they wish.

Many initiatives take a different tack. They start with some form of consumer or community service, from social events to social action. Then, having developed networks of trust, individuals are invited to a further group, in which Christianity is explored. The explicitly Christian element is kept separate from the original group.

Some youth churches are exploring this model. One approach is to help young people acquire a qualification or a dance group to prepare for a performance, or to offer courses for young people wanting to make a CD or film. From each group or course a cell might form for those who want to explore health or other issues. The hope is that the cell will be a setting in which to raise spiritual questions. Perhaps it will gradually evolve into an expression of church.

Whether they start with a Christian dimension at the beginning or seek to introduce it later, the key is discovering what will work for the group. Being stimulated and inspired by the experience of others may help practitioners discern what is appropriate for the group – hence the need to connect, collect and reflect.

Connecting

A nightmare future is that scores of fresh expressions emerge over the next decade, but they remain isolated, wither away and leave inherited church profoundly disillusioned, with no obvious strategy to reverse its marginalization.

This could happen if pioneers fail to link up with each other, or form ad hoc support groups rather than intentional learning networks. Connections would be warm and encouraging, but the amount of learning – from disappointments as well as 'successes' – would be limited. Practitioners would keep inventing the wheel, they would repeat the same mistakes and knowledge about how best to approach fresh expressions would grow painfully slowly.

Part of the nightmare would be that new expressions of church fail to connect with each other and with inherited forms of church. New believers would have a narrow experience of church that would stunt their spiritual growth. A significant number would become bored and leave. Or an individual's circumstances might change – perhaps they start to work a new shift so that they can no longer attend on Thursday evenings. They drop out rather than find their way to another expression of church.

Good practice for fresh expressions will include prioritizing links with other parts of the church. Pioneers will join learning networks and emerging believers will be given opportunities to make contact with the wider Christian community.

There are dozens of ways of joining Christians together – from short evening courses run on a deanery basis, to weekend retreats with other churches, to parish social events involving several expressions of the local church, to pilgrimages or Greenbelt-type events, to parish or inter-denominational holidays, to web-based expressions of church. Which approaches will work best? Practitioners need to learn from each other to discover the answers.

Historically, working together has been one the Church's biggest struggles. Is 'connecting up' a council of perfection? Perhaps not:

- In today's 'network society', more and more people find it natural to make connections. Scarcely anyone belongs to just one network. The emerging nature of society will make it easy for believers, as they mature, to belong to several Christian networks, perhaps spanning several expressions of church. As learning networks proliferate in the wider society, leaders of fresh expressions will not be surprised to be invited to join networks with an explicit learning purpose.

- In our 'mosaic' culture, individuals increasingly do not think in terms of 'either-or' but 'both-and'. They don't want to be locked into one group: they want the freedom to join several, quite similar groups at the same time. 'Boutique churches' are beginning to emerge, whereby individuals belong to more than one church. Some church leaders may find that this takes a bit of getting used to. But as the trend accelerates, it could create opportunities for new Christians to be more widely connected.

- Most people are less certain about truth than in the past. More relaxed attitudes to truth raise theological questions, but they do have one advantage: they mean most churchgoers are less concerned about denominational differences. This may make it easier for local churches to pool their resources, despite differences in churchmanship and tradition – 'we've got a gifted couple who would be prepared to organize marriage preparation for the town. We would be very happy to leave it to you to organize Christian discipleship courses, and we would certainly join in with you if you arranged a children's holiday club.'

- The fragile state of the Church in many areas is already forcing many local churches to work together, and the number doing this could grow.

Conclusion

Any choice of issues in good practice is bound to be somewhat arbitrary and invite complaints, 'Why have you left out developing mission-shaped values?'

'What about discipleship?' 'Shouldn't you have said something about sustaining fragile expressions?' . . .

The truth is that we do not yet have adequate answers to many of these questions, including some of the tasks discussed above. We are in the midst of a prolonged period of experimentation and learning in which, through the sharing of wisdom, the Church as a whole is discovering what works well in which contexts. That is one reason why processes for accumulating wisdom in fresh expressions are so important. They will enable lessons from experimentation to be learnt.

Experimentation necessarily involves disappointments. This means there needs to be not only patience, but generosity on the part of the wider Church, so that pioneers are given time and space both to demonstrate the potential of being church in new and different ways and also to make their mistakes. However, if we can build in new methods of shared learning, maybe pioneers will make the same mistake only once!

Pioneers in turn owe it to each other and to the wider Church to share what they are learning so that their journeys can become other people's journeys too. Huge opportunities lie ahead. Can the Church develop new ways of learning and sharing to make the most of them?

9

Mapping the mixed economy[1]

Ann Morisy

Ann Morisy is a community worker and theologian, currently working in London. She is the author of Beyond the Good Samaritan *(1997) and* Journeying Out *(2004). In this chapter Ann explores a different kind of map and develops a language for the mixed economy Church rooted in her experience of transformation, discipleship and community.*

Since the report *Mission-shaped Church* was published and the Archbishop of Canterbury, Rowan Williams, spoke of a 'mixed economy' of churches, there is a need for a map to help make sense of the burgeoning new ways of being church. The terrain that such a map needs to cover is the multiplicity of effort being made to make God credible, 'visible' and accessible to post-Enlightenment, cynical and anxious people, that is, people of Britain in the twenty-first century. I suggest that by constructing a map with three domains it becomes possible to locate many of the current initiatives, and, importantly, locate 'lacunae' or gaps that are still to be populated. The three domains are:

- the explicit domain;
- the foundational domain;
- the vocational or invitational domain.

The explicit domain

Work in the explicit domain is focused on enabling people to have confidence that God is with us in Jesus and that Jesus' teachings carry authority. Most of our church practice is geared to the explicit domain, which is characterized by public worship, organized around the formularies of the Christian faith, and shaped by the diverse, but explicit expressions of particular churchmanship and denomination. However, the explicit domain now presents a threshold that is too high for many people to cross. Our 'inherited mode' of being church is so complex and inaccessible that people are anxious about crossing that threshold. Or the recited formularies of the faith are seen as so implausible or impenetrable that Sunday by Sunday church fails to engage with people.

It would be a mistake to dismiss the explicit domain as being the home of anachronistic practices that can be allowed to wither on the branch. The explicit domain is at the centre of the map, for it is here that the significance of Jesus is unfurled in all its fullness and the wisdom of generations of Christians is distilled. The issue is not one of redundancy. In fact, an increasing number of theologians (in particular, Stanley Hauerwas, John Milbank and other proponents of Radical Orthodoxy) suggest that by enhancing commitment to the explicit domain the Christian community can become a subversive force which can model new ways of social policy and social relationship to bring greater congruence with God's promises for his creation.

The difficulty with the explicit domain is not just that of obscurity. The high symbolic nature of much of church life is at odds with the earthbound symbols that dominate our culture. Even the linguistic codes of popular culture rarely encourage people to lift their eyes above the horizon in order to sense the holy or to recognize the felt presence of God that is potentially ours. In a materialistic, earth-bound culture we have to do preliminary work before people can contemplate the presence of God, let alone worship. The challenge is to widen the approach to the explicit domain in order that its value can be recognized and sustained for future generations. The purpose of the foundational and vocational (or invitational) domains is to widen access to the explicit domain rather than undermine it. However, to do this calls for resources to be shifted from the explicit domain, which over the centuries has been the primary focus of church resources.

The foundational domain

The task in the foundational domain is to strengthen people's confidence in their intimation that there is an enduring spiritual reality. This has to involve more than responding to low levels of religious literacy, essentially it involves helping to foster within people *a sense of the possibility of God*. This task is new. Never before have churches had to work to 're-enchant' people's view of the world. One of the consequences of the Enlightenment has been a literal disenchantment with so many aspects of life in northern Europe.[2] People now have to be given permission and support if they are to have confidence in their sense of the presence of God. This foundation is essential if as a Church we are to be able to preach and teach 'God Incarnate'.

Chaplains: pioneers of the foundational domain

Pioneering work in the foundational domain has been undertaken for many decades by chaplains – whether in hospitals, prisons, the Armed Forces, industry or colleges. Essentially chaplains are involved in a ministry of awakening, and are practised in the courage of beginning conversations of the spirit which enable people, however haltingly, to explore their sense of there being more to life than meets the eye. The chaplain also has the skill of code-switching which enables the clumsy efforts to express sub-Christian ideas to be treated respectfully and accorded value. The opportunity to proffer a concept from an informed Christian perspective, to go alongside homespun insights, may present itself but can never be forced, for to do so would be to breach the hospitality that is at the heart of the chaplain's task. Such inclusiveness is a vital component of the foundational domain. For in this domain hospitality has to be shown to everyone – regardless of how quirky their beliefs and spiritual habits might be.

Visible unity

Ecumenism has long been understood as an aspect of mission. The disunity of churches provides a good excuse for keeping out of the explicit domain, where the *club accretions* of churchmanship and denomination are most visible. However, the level of disinterest in church life is such that the impact of disunity has become less significant, with people no longer even aware of the differences between denominations. But unity now matters in a different way. All of us have a longing for solidarity. In the past solidarity has usually been between blood relatives, those from the same village or town and of the same ethnicity / nationality. However, in a globalizing world people have become acutely aware, not just of difference but of fragmentation, and this is a disconcerting dynamic. The experience of diversity and fragmentation is at minimum disorientating, for others it can be grievous. In this new context, solidarity, not just across denomination, but across age and sex and ethnicity provides positive symbols that can have a very positive impact.

One of the dominant narratives that shapes people's attitudes is Samuel Huntington's notion of the idea of the clash of civilizations – i.e. the clash between Islam and Christianity.[3] This increases suspicion that religion is a dangerous force. It is essential, therefore, to demonstrate that Christians and Muslims can live together and work together for the well-being of others. In the public domain the solidarity of people from across faiths becomes a powerful witness that is vitally important to the foundational domain.

Haringey, like a number of London Boroughs, has an infamous 'murder mile' where gun violence has become almost routine. Under the leadership of the Revd Nims Obunge, the churches in the borough meet to pray and walk the patch. Their prayers are for social peace and healing between people. From this, the Haringey Peace Alliance developed, and this group gave birth to the London Peace Alliance. The Peace Alliance invites all people, not just Christians, to gather in solidarity. This includes Muslims and representatives of the local mosques. The foundational domain calls Christians to forego talks of (say) a Christian Alliance, in order to reach for the inclusiveness that becomes possible with a *peace* alliance.

Church centres?

Over the last 20 years more and more churches have adapted their buildings to enable their use by the wider community. While this is good stewardship of resources, it is questionable how effective community use of church buildings is in relation to the foundational domain – and the vital task of 'giving birth to God in the soul'. In particular, the problem of perception gets underestimated. Potentially, those from the wider community can assume that the adapted buildings are a sign that the Church has gone into an irreversible decline, or that the Church needs to make money from the rent, or that the local authority or residents' association has taken over the premises because the Church has quit.

To be effective in relation to the foundational domain the challenge is to enable those who use or visit the centre to come away feeling that they have received *more* than they had expected, that is, to have received a blessing. This, together with helping people to lift their eyes above the mundane, is a task that needs to be part of the repertoire of churches committed to community involvement. Such precise tasks, which are part of the foundational domain, are important preparation for the explicit domain, and call for a deliberate strategy in relation to the adaptation and opening-up of church buildings and, in particular, call for a new role – that of *community chaplain*. This role can be undertaken by trained volunteers. It may be that a church has two or three community chaplains, just as happens with readers or lay preachers.

The first task of a community chaplain is to call in regularly on the groups using the church centre or hall, and to do this with a view to:

- encouraging people to 'do business with God';
- bringing greater integration of Sunday church life with the week-day activities;
- presenting the church centre as a new *way of being church*, countering the idea that the church centre represents the church rationalizing its resources or wanting to generate income;
- building a sense of belonging and 'feeling at home' by centre users.

The role of community chaplain involves being *priest for the everyday*, that is, representing, and occasionally speaking about, God's alongsideness in relation to daily life – whether the moment is filled with delight, stress or struggle. However, it is important that the role does not drift into pastoral care as the role of community chaplain is primarily about ministering *to groups* rather than individuals. The challenge at the heart of the role is to create and maintain a porous and delicate membrane that prevents caring and being alongside drifting into controlling and shaping. The community chaplain has to let go of any desire to shape or control how people think, both about their neighbours and about God. To breach or destroy this membrane would be to cut across the hospitality which the Church Centre has to represent.

Apt liturgy

In particular, the community chaplain needs to be alert to opportunities for apt liturgy which can engage with the struggles, and on occasion the hopes, of that community, beginning with those who are part of the groups using the church centre. Encouragement to offer apt liturgy to the wider community comes from the work of Grace Davie. As explored in Chapter 3, her extensive research suggests that in Britain, and to a large extent in Europe, we have developed 'vicarious religion', that is, religion performed by an active minority but on behalf of a much larger number, who at some deep level are pleased that the minority are committed to maintaining a religious practice and culture.[4] This sympathy with religion is an asset in relation to the foundational domain, and makes possible 'apt liturgy' that provides a context in which to introduce elements which are important to the explicit domain.

Often apt liturgy takes place outside the church building,[5] although the apt liturgy offered for the people of Soham in 2002, when faced with the murder of two young girls in their community, made good use of the church building and the symbolic resonances with eternity that the building offered. Apt liturgy is different from the worship that takes place in the explicit domain because it is designed for those who only half-believe, or have inchoate beliefs – those who are struggling with the possibility of God. Apt liturgy calls for immense courage and emotional literacy on the part of those who dare to design and host the liturgy – or event – to use more secular terminology.[6] It involves identifying the situation that provokes strong emotion, acting with sensitivity, creativity and at speed to offer the liturgy to those for whom religion is normally 'vicarious', and the role of community chaplain provides the necessary alertness to such opportunities that provide a context through which the 'cairns' that are critical to the journey towards Christian faith[7] can be introduced:

These cairns include:

- Generating a sense of solidarity between people in their struggle and introducing the possibility that God also shares in that struggle. Helping people to embrace the sense of God being in solidarity with them is an important foundation for the 'tall story' of the incarnation.

- Introducing the reality that all of us fall short – that to 'mess-up' is the norm, no one is exempt. Part of being human is to be vulnerable and to feel frail. Fostering recognition of such realities is an essential foundation for the explicit domain where there is open acknowledgment of our need for a saviour.

- Telling a story about, or from Jesus, enables the subversive perspective of Jesus to be seen, countering the popular idea that Jesus is meek and mild, all right for children but not grown-ups. In a time when political ideologies are discredited, the radicalness of the way in which Jesus lived his life is both attractive and refreshing to those who find belief in a personal God difficult.

- Enabling a movement from struggle and dismay to that of fortitude and hope is an important aspect of apt liturgy. Giving an account of the hope and strength that stirs within energises the consideration of the 'possibility' of God.

- Creating memories of the heart that can be pondered over time and drawn on and built on through a lifetime.

While it is possible to construct apt liturgy around positive events such as community celebrations it is in relation to tough 'communal' emotions that apt liturgy best furthers the work of the foundational domain. Helping people to move from a state of dismay to one of hope and solidarity has always been a function of the Church. However, as life became more amiable and reliance on personal prowess and material efficacy grew (all of which are products of the Enlightenment), a heavenly basis for hope became redundant. The growing number of gridlocks and dysfunctions in technology and human design means that confidence in human enterprise is increasingly questioned. This change from a utopian to a more dystopian perspective means that the messages carried through apt liturgy have growing potency.

The vocational domain

The vocational domain is the third aspect of the map. It is this terrain that has been explored least, but that may hold the greatest potential for holistic mission, linking work for the kingdom of God with recognition of salvation through Jesus. The vocational or invitational domain is about encouraging people – both those inside the Church and out – to discover and embrace their distinctive call from God. This domain relies on the assumption that everyone has within them an urge to be a better self. Furthermore, by enabling people to heed and respond to this calling within them, this in turn enables people to *discover* love of neighbour, both close at hand and further afield, and to discover God incarnate – who is also close at hand.

The vocational domain is essentially about discipleship. Karl Rahner describes discipleship as venturesome love, emphasizing that discipleship involves an element of risk.[8] However, the resource greedy explicit domain often degrades discipleship into helping to run a church – to the extent that the normative model of how one expresses deeper commitment to God is by ever greater involvement in running the Church. This can often be at the expense of *risk taking* for the sake of the well-being of others.

Work in the vocational domain involves encouraging people to develop or 'craft' a 'better self'. This involves inviting people to express concern and commitment to others beyond the limits of their family or household or likeminded others. This encouragement to encounter the stranger as brother or sister is an essential aspect of the vocational domain, if it is to be of service to the explicit domain. The means of delivering these objectives is by inviting people to engage in processes that will bring about an encounter with *the face of the other*, in the expectation that this will be a profound and potentially transforming experience.

At a minimum, the vocational domain aims at provoking within each person an internal conversation, prompted by the invitation to (say) meet asylum seekers as they arrive in town having been dispersed from London, or help with a temporary winter night shelter for homeless people. Such invitations are essential to the vocational domain because they trigger an internal conversation 'Could I?', 'Should I?' These are questions that go right to the heart of vocational and moral behaviour. Such heart-felt pondering should not be underestimated, because it indicates a hesitation, an anxiety about one's capacity to cope. It indicates that the person is on the brink of 'Openness to experience as well as to criticism; and a sensitivity and responsiveness to the needs and concerns of others.'[9] The internal conversation 'Could I?' 'Should I?' speaks of hesitation about one's ability in relation to the invitation, and this state of mind is critical to the vocational domain for it makes us ready for inner reassessment and inner re-arrangement and the associated openness to new learning and information.

The invitation to come alongside those who are intimately acquainted with struggle can be distressing and even harrowing, particularly when without power. Even without such potentially challenging encounters, responding positively to the invitation confronts us with the unfamiliar, and therefore interrupts our sense of being in control. In looking into the face of the old woman with dementia we see our own potential self. Listening without power to the man struggling with schizophrenia as he expresses his confidence in God's protection provokes an internal conversation within the listener, to which he or she will likely return on many occasions. Inviting the suburban husband and wife to journey to Asmara provokes within each of them an internal conversation that forces them to confront their inclination to be timid – or courageous. Seeing the face of the asylum seeker who is alone in a strange land evokes within us recognition of our own vulnerability and our shared need for belonging. By allowing ourselves to be without power in a challenging situation or encounter, we open ourselves to *a thin place*, where something new and something with a moral imperative can intrude.

Religious experience

It was George McLeod, the modern day founder of the Iona Community who coined the term 'thin place' to describe the special quality of the isle – where only a 'tissue separates you from an awareness of God'. The experience of being without power and facing up to the possibility of being overwhelmed is likewise a thin place, which can trigger a religious experience as our usual capacities and coping techniques are challenged:

- Religious experience is often triggered by the anxiety associated with being overwhelmed (through a sudden challenge or demand or a crisis of some kind).
- The vocational domain is about risking or even practising being overwhelmed.
- Religious experience opens people to a transforming encounter with God.

- This transformation takes the following form:
  - a greater confidence in God's alongsideness in daily life
  - a greater sense of being at home in the world
  - a greater commitment to 'moral' behaviour.

This equation is compelling because it illustrates how holistic mission can flow in a way that can only be described as a cascading of grace. Intuitively we know that the kingdom of God will come, not through more and more hard work by hard pressed Christians, but by 'doing it like Jesus'. In allowing our selves, and enabling others, to face up to the possibility of being overwhelmed and to be without power, we do the same as Jesus did in his life. And when we do as Jesus did we experience God-given blessings that cannot be numbered. One of these blessings is that our mission becomes holistic,[10] in that it furthers the kingdom of God – and enables people to encounter God. The vocational domain, therefore, by encouraging and enabling people to express discipleship, regardless of whether they are Christian, overthrows the usual 'belonging, believing, behaving' formula. The presumption is that, by encouraging people to express venturesome love, a *route* to faith is created, rather than assuming that venturesome love can only be expressed by Christians.

The democratic fact of life: all have sinned

There is an inherent inequality in the encounter between the poor and struggling with the *apparently* secure and confident that needs to be acknowledged. Therefore it is essential that opportunities are available for people to reflect on their experiences and their encounters, not least because through this reflection comes an awareness of our sinfulness, for in relation to sinfulness there is equality. While there may be an inequality in relation to power and status there is no such inequality in relation to sin: *all* have sinned and fallen short. Recognition of this democratic fact of life is an important aspect of the vocational or invitational domain, because unless an awareness of sinfulness is fostered the need for salvation is irrelevant – and so too is the explicit domain.

The growth in awareness of our sinfulness comes from seeing things from the perspective of the excluded and downtrodden. The battle against addiction takes on a heroic nature when witnessed close-up; from close-up the young prostitute is recognized as more abused than immoral. The act of turning away a homeless man from the night shelter because it is full breaks one's heart. Rather than becoming confident in one's own good works the likelihood is that awareness grows that 'There but for the grace of God go I'. Personal sins and inadequacies are scarcely different between the well heeled and the down at heel. Furthermore, awareness of one's complicity in sinful systems grows. Those who benefit most from welfare provision are those who administer it, no matter how much effort goes in to make it otherwise. However this pattern of advantage has to be seen in order to be believed.

Saunders and Campbell, both of whom are professors in theology who chose to spend a sabbatical working as volunteers in shelters for the homeless, comment that until this experience they had: 'Assumed that discipleship followed the confession of sin and the acceptance of forgiveness. The faltering hospitality offered via the basement door has taught that the process is actually reversed: we do not fully know the depth of our sin and the reality of God's grace until we follow the way of Jesus.'[11] In this observation they articulate the significance of the vocational domain: It is a route to recognizing our need for a saviour. At this point the work of the explicit domain takes over, because the message of forgiveness and the message of salvation are able to be heard – and welcomed.

How realistic is all this?

If the vocational domain can support the explicit domain as effectively as this, the issue becomes that of feasibility. Is it realistic to work in this way? Would people respond to an invitation? The answer is a resounding 'Yes'. We are in the midst of a kairos moment – a decisive moment – because the invitation to become a better self is *precisely* what the marketing industry says people are wanting. In their epoch-making book, *The Experience Economy*, Pine and Gilmore write, 'This is new: experiences represent an existing but previously unarticulated *genre of economic output.*'[12] The newness that they refer to is the shift from the marketing and promotion of commodities to that of marketing experiences.

In the West, the market for 'stuff' has reached saturation. In this emerging experience economy the more a business can create an experience that engages people in a personal and memorable way the more that business will be successful. Most churches would feel that this is *their* very intention. Furthermore, Pine and Gilmore reckon the experience of transformation – that is, to become a better person – to be the 'economic output' that is most prized. Once again, most churches would say this is their very intention. Marketing experts would suggest, therefore, that people are more than ready to embrace the vocational domain with its potential for transformation.

The work we do in the vocational domain taps into the urge for transformation and the associated urge to develop a story-rich life. So, in marketing terms, the annual pilgrimage between London and Canterbury organized by St Martin's in the Field for both homeless and housed boasts on its flier 'Once you've done it, you just have to come back next year . . . and the next . . . and the next.' The pilgrimage offers that *sweet spot* that marketing experts long for. What is on offer is a combination of convivial partnership, easy-going spirituality and it carries a story rich potential. The offer of partaking in a 'bank holiday weekend of a lifetime' is precisely the kind of *pre-formative experience* that *fortifies the aspirant* to continue to *clarify the nature of the transformation* that he or she seeks.

There are other examples of *pre-formative experiences* that churches and church related agencies are starting to develop. Camden in North London is perhaps the most expressively post modern location in Britain.[13] The churches in the borough have had to adapt themselves to this market-leading community. Ten years ago at St Michael's Camden Town, the congregation was down to single figures, now the congregation is vibrant and Camden Town is aware that the local church is relevant and as full of life as the community itself. The church invites people from the congregation and from the wider community to participate in events and encounters that provoke the important internal conversation 'Could I?' 'Should I?' So it may be the asylum seeker who cooks for the homeless; the Camden-based opera singer or artist who accepts an invitation to run opera and singing workshops with the Somali young people, and other local artists likewise. All the opportunities and events have a low threshold, providing taster experiences that speak of the potential transformation (crafting a better self) that is on offer through participation.

St George the Martyr in Bloomsbury has also faced the challenge of building up its congregation and re-awakening the neighbourhood to its presence. Here the approach has been to muster energy for just the single week, daring to suggest to the congregation that they should take a week off work and use their holiday to run activities and events within the parish. Old people's flats are spring cleaned, kitchens are painted, after school football tournaments hosted and invitations issued to hear a couple of bands at the 'St George' the new 'local'. The 'Wave' which also gives scope for people from local businesses and local residents to participate, is repeated at least once a year, and this fulfils a further insight from the world of marketing: Pine and Gilmore comment 'By staging a series of experiences (companies) are better able to achieve a lasting effect on the buyer, than through an isolated event. It is the revisiting of a recurring theme, experienced through distinct and yet unified events that transforms.'[14]

The Soul Survivor movement also achieves this careful staging of experiences. Over 10,000 young people gather each year in a major city, forming teams to clear rubbish, remove graffiti, tidy gardens and party and pray in the evening. This initiative meets all the criteria of transformational experiences that Pine and Gilmore identify plus one more: Soul in the City creates a 'line of memorability'[15] for the participants. That line of memorability will have to compete with the line of memorability generated by backpacking in Peru and working in a hotel in St Ives for six weeks over the summer. These will be the experiences that are recounted in the students' bar and feed young people's internal conversations that inform their choices in the future.

The episodic, pre-formative events that I have described above take account of the vast number of competing models of life that people can choose, and they can do much to rehabilitate people's view of the Church. But they do more than this, they provide a glimpse of a better self, which is both moral, in that it seeks to express wider fraternal relations, and also leads to a story rich life. These episodic, participative events provide material that people can use to create a cohering life story. At some stage in our lives we sense the superficiality of personality and begin to recognize the value and significance of *character*. Character resides in aspiring to *maintain* an ideal, and self respect depends on this.[16] Episodic events need to make room for more consistent expression of our moral selves if we are to both develop character and sustain the transformation that is being sought.

There have been very successful initiatives that have given people the opportunity to sustain transformation: The Salvation Army and the Catholic Worker Movement (established by Dorothy Day in the USA) are perhaps the best known. We need to revisit their approach in order to increase the work that we do in relation to the vocational domain. Mission societies could partner local churches to enable new structures of participation to be developed, and to devise ways to ensure that the transformation once achieved does not degenerate. Attending to this follow-through phase gives a fresh agenda for the extensive home groups, cell churches and fellowship groups that currently are orientated solely towards the explicit domain.

Discussion questions

What do you think are the resource implications of developing the vocational and foundational domains? To what extent do you consider the explicit domain to be 'resource greedy'?

Do you sense that people have an urge to be a better self?

The majority of adults in Britain can relate an experience they have had which they describe as 'religious'. In the past, religious experience has tended to be underplayed by the Church because it gives people personal confidence in God that can threaten the authority of the Church. Now that our church life is not about authority is there scope to be more hospitable to religious experience?

10

Fresh expressions growing to maturity

George Lings

George Lings is Director of the Church Army's Sheffield Centre and author of the Encounters on the Edge *series of studies on fresh expressions of church. George was a member of the working party that produced* Mission-shaped Church. *He writes of the complex nature of Christian maturity and its application to developing fresh expressions of church.*

Why does it matter that fresh expressions mature?

Tactical reasons

As this book has argued, in the Church of England there is now a 'mixed economy';[1] we have a growing number of fresh expressions of church alongside previous expressions. Some are suspicious that the recent arrivals are just a restless search for relevance or being trendy. Others ask, 'Do they compromise the nature of church and take resources away from it?' Yet our denomination's instinct for diversity has given permission and space to the fresh expressions. Will they justify that trust?

The concern in Scripture

There is a wide textual base in the New Testament that is interested in the maturity of Christians and churches. The parables of Jesus show an interest in fruitfulness. A classic case would be the parable of the sower; that sown among thorns does not mature (Luke 8.14). Part of Jesus' prophetic action was to curse an unfruitful fig tree. Paul holds out a vision of maturity to the churches in Corinth (1 Corinthians 14.30), Ephesus (Ephesians 4.13), Philippi (Philippians 3.15) and Colossae (Colossians 1.28). The specific context is maturity of mind, but the wider issues of the letters broaden it to ethical and communal maturity. Both John and Paul urge the community to grow towards being perfected in love. James is critical of actions not matching faith and of a tongue that betrays a lack of maturity. The letters to the seven churches are critical of failures to mature in faith, love and action. Perhaps in Colossians we are given the fulcrum of this passion that Christians grow into maturity in Christ (Colossians 1.28).

The theological support

Behind the texts are themes that buttress reasons for the significance and importance of maturity. The covenant and the prophets share a concern that the glory of God is diminished if his people fail to live out covenant values in their worship, community dealings, treatment of the poor and aliens, and in their domestic lives. In terms of the Trinity, the lack of maturity dishonours the Father, whose intention is that we become the beloved with whom he is well pleased. Maturity misrepresents the Son, for we are called by his name. Lack of maturity grieves the Spirit who dwells within us. In terms of ecclesiology, a lack of maturity hinders the Church in its call to be an authentic sign of the kingdom, acting as light or salt. Lack of maturity will compromise the mission of the church, as its witness to the world is diluted, contradictory and even counter productive. Yet all these concerns apply generically to every expression of church. Indeed, it is the widespread reproach over our past failures that provides one motivation towards the creation of fresh expressions. People sense 'there must be more than this'.

People reasons

Without growth to maturity, those sent out to create fresh expressions of church can become disillusioned and exhausted. Immature communities will also be alienating to spiritual searchers and cynical watchers. Those who become Christians through fresh expressions of church stand in danger of losing their faith. Resources invested in the calling, training and deploying of pioneer leaders could be wasted. The passion of pioneers and the wisdom of the permission givers needs to create an environment which believes that starting is not enough; there are important issues of sustainability. Starting is no guarantee of finishing. Again the parables of Jesus underline this reality; take the receiving of talents or the person wanting to build towers (Matthew 25.14-30; Luke 14.28-30). Maturity matters.

What is maturity?

Confusions: what it is not

The usage of language of maturity about human beings may be helpful and even revealing.

- Maturity is not the same as old, staid or safe. For example, it is meaningful to speak of a mature nine-year-old. Maturity is relative to expectations and stages.
- Maturity is neither the same as being sophisticated, nor directly related to size or power.
- While adulthood is theoretically conferred with age and voting status, by no means all adults behave in mature ways.
- In the human domain not all that is old is mature – there are crabby, immature elderly people. Though longevity is a sign of blessing in the Old Testament, the New seems more interested in character, relationship and fruitfulness.
- Maturity is not necessarily becoming like your parents. It is growing into what you are.

If this is true, then in church life many factors that have long been thought of as conferring respectable, possibly authentic, Anglican identity may not be measures of maturity. Maturity is not directly related to either the age of the worship building used, or the legal status of the church, or even its parish responsibility. It neither comes automatically with the theological sophistication or size of congregation, nor the seniority of the leader. It is not intrinsically linked to how long people have been church in a place. It is to be hoped that experience and responsibility assist maturity, but there are plenty of examples where it does not – ask any archdeacon. Insisting that in external features Fresh Expressions must look just like previous expressions does not seem to be any direct measure worth using.

Suggestions: what human maturity is

- It is a relational quality that holds various dimensions of being human in creative tension and enables stances to be taken, and decisions made, that are appropriate.
- Maturity holds together dealing well with others and with oneself; it is aware of circumstances and reactions to them.
- Maturity has a sense of what is desirable, what is possible and of what is yet unknown.

- It balances love and truth, compassion and judgement. It is able to commit to words and actions and to sustain those initiatives in a responsible way.
- It operates beyond demeaning dependence and fierce independence. It is strongly linked to healthy interdependence, which can only grow as the two previous stages are handled well.[2]
- At the same time it is relative to age, experience and resources.

Why should human maturity be any indicator of church maturity?

- Relationships within the Trinity offer us a vision of mature, interpersonal and interconnected life. The fact that humans are fashioned in the image of God connects us to these values.[3]
- The restoring of the image of God is central to the longer processes of salvation. This encompasses relationships with God, other people and creation. In those senses it is said that the glory of God is a human being fully alive.[4] The Church on earth is at best a foretaste of these realities.
- Some images of the Church (People of God, Body of Christ, Second Adam, New Creation) connect back to the first two factors. These strengthen links between how God is, his purpose and what it is to be human.
- The loving self-giving nature of God is reflected in the calling of the Church. Some argue that the mark of the Church is love,[5] drawing on the example and commands of Christ. Love without maturity could be merely romantic or even self-centred.

Measuring maturity is not an MOT test

It would be foreign to the Anglican spirit of inclusion to construct such a rigorous set of demands and standards that tended to disbar or disenfranchise young churches. A pass–fail system will not help us, especially one like the MOT that fails a whole vehicle on the fault in one of its parts. Rather the culture of appraisal might help. We need to nurture the aspiration for values and instincts that lead to maturity in churches. As such a 'good enough' theology, that praises a desire to be on this road, could be quite enough to ask. In addition what is asked of emerging churches should be applied also to existing ones.

How might maturity be seen in a fresh expression of church?

All assessments need to fit the age and stage of the expression. Behaviour and a sense of identity considered mature in a child, teenager, young adult, are not the same. Intention may be as significant as achievement. Being church seems to be the result of what happens when people encounter Jesus in such a way that it transforms them to become more like him and so also transforms their relationships with one another.[6] In one sense maturity is the process of growing up into Christ, becoming in practice what by change of status we already are. It is a long, undulating process with spiritual, moral and social dimensions. Maturity is connected to integrity and authenticity, for mature behaviour and reactions have a health, balance and cohesion that are attractive. It is also linked to awareness of self-identity and self-knowledge. So churches that demonstrate maturity will also have a good idea of what church is, what it is for and what it is like when healthy.

As Graham Cray argues more fully, *Mission-shaped Church* identifies some useful indicators, all of which have a part to play in assessing maturity and which need to speak to one another.

The four historic marks: one, holy, apostolic and catholic

However, the disturbing tale alongside these venerable marks of the Church is that the history of Church doctrine reveals different interpretations of all of them. Very often the changes were made for polemical reasons. The self-understanding of the Church has often evolved through periods of conflict,[7] thus the meaning of the marks is not entirely agreed.

One example could suffice. The meaning of the term Catholic has shifted several times. The earliest use by Ignatius meant *the whole church of a particular place*. Under Cyprian, over a century later, it came to mean *universal*, and used to counter the regional claims of the Donatist group. During the Reformation it became a label of approval or abuse. It changed also because the fracturing of the western Christian Church into Protestant and Roman camps denied universality to both groups. Archbishop Michael Ramsay engagingly admitted: 'I believe passionately in the one holy catholic and apostolic Church and very much regret that it does not exist.' In common parlance today it can be shorthand for high church styles of worship and an emphasis on the threefold orders of ministry: bishops, priests and deacons.

In *Mission-shaped Church*, the elements of wholeness and universality are held in the time frame of the completion of all things in a new heaven and earth, when true universality, wholeness and inclusion will be finally realized. This reminds us that before then all expressions of catholicity are only partial and that *a journey towards inclusivity* is another part of being catholic. Thus it becomes clear that the word has been used in a variety of ways.

Catholicity is also presented as one of four journeys that need to be made by every expression of church.[8] It is the journey into interdependence with other expressions of church. This way of looking at catholicity fits well with maturity. The catholic journey reminds every expression, fresh or previous, that it does not exist by itself, nor for itself. This reality should be very clear to all planted churches, for normally they have a sending church and a group to which they are sent. It should be normal thinking for Anglicans who exist in a Communion, with provinces, dioceses and congregations. Church is held to be more than local. However the writing of non-Anglicans in the church planting field makes very little of this dimension and can reinforce an ecclesiology of congregationalism.

Yet it is probably this mark of the Church, rather than it being one, holy, or apostolic, which most fully connects to the important progression to maturity, for that is a quality intrinsically connected to seeing ourselves in relation to others who are not the same as us. It has been quite possible for an expression of church to be fiercely independent about its oneness as local unity, its holiness as spiritual or moral excellence and apostolic effectiveness in mission. The attendant ignorance of other churches, or lack of humility in relating to them, then becomes a reproach and shows some lack of maturity over catholicity.

If a propensity to ignore the interdependent nature of church being catholic is a temptation to fresh expressions, then, in my view, the tendency of previous expressions has been to play down the apostolic dimension. I do not mean they ignore their historical origins, which is one way in which being apostolic is understood. Rather, I mean their tendency is to fail to see their community identity as being sent; linguistically the root theological meaning of the word 'apostle'. Too many existing churches are not mission-minded, let alone mission-shaped. As such there are significant questions over their maturity in that their life could often be described as self-centred and preoccupied with their internal affairs.

Maturity is an issue for all churches. As maturity is always dynamically related to circumstances, maturity will not necessarily be an even and gradual growth in these four dimensions at the same time. The art of such growth may be more a discerning, across the four journeys, that is to be developed in any given season:

- an upward facing dimension seeking God to become more like him in his *holiness*;
- an inward facing dimension growing a community that reflects the diverse *oneness* of the Trinity;

- an outward facing dimension that embodies the *apostolic* community living out being sent;
- an all round facing dimension – seeing the expression as only part of the *catholic* wider whole.

On reflection it may be helpful to say that the fresh expressions face the danger of failing to look *back and around* to learn from the wider Church, while the rest of the western church fails to look *out* to the world to which it is sent. In the mixed economy, learning from one another's mistakes beckons.

Marks of maturing learnt from the world Church

Mission-shaped Church draws on the nineteenth-century thought of Henry Venn and his experiences of overseas mission, which indicate that 'native churches' too often failed to thrive. They remained worryingly dependent on foreign subsidy and leadership. If, as *Mission-shaped Church* argues, the reality of home mission is now cross cultural, there is additional reason to turn to these lessons once more.

The so-called '*three self principles*' are that churches started should move as rapidly as possible to the state of being self-governing, self-financing and self-propagating. The last is often also called self-reproducing. The three are linked. Self-government will be enabled or frustrated by the ability to be self-financing and both are tested by fruitfulness in self-propagation.

How should this work in practice? The young Church becomes indigenous, shaped by the engagement of the mission with the culture. Part of this is shown by the emergence of indigenous leadership, who embody and facilitate the three dimensions of growth to maturity. This emergence is itself also one sign of self-propagation. Any organism that produces its own leaders is exhibiting a sign of health and of maturing. One of the challenges to the maturity of the rest of the church is how readily it can accept these leaders and the patterns in their churches, which may well take forms that are different from previous expressions.[9] If the task is cross-cultural, and the expressions grow from the process of enculturation, this needs to be expected. Inflexibility is not a mark of maturity. Mission-shaped churches would look different from Christendom-cloned churches.

It should be noted that Venn, leader of CMS in the mid-nineteenth century, did not see 'three self growth' as a passage to independence, or a disconnection from the principle of episcopacy. Rather, he looked for a progression from disabling dependence, through independence, into interdependence in the Anglican family. However, it has to be said that this theory has always exceeded the ability of the wider Church to let it happen. Even by the 1880s it was only honoured in theory. In practice cultural imperialism and local collusion with it were once more dominant. In the Edwardian period Roland Allen argued for the re-establishment of this way of thinking and rooted his case in Pauline practice. He highlighted theological dynamics that must undergird the three developments. He spoke of trust in the Holy Spirit and trust in the people. These elements clash – both with benign attempts to control and with the darker suspicion that the depravity of human beings is so deep that new Christians are not to be trusted. His writing too is much admired but practised less than it is applauded.

It looks as though marks of maturity are well known, but too often there is lack of trust and freedom for these marks to flourish in an indigenous fresh expression. The best practical remedy is building trusting relationships between pioneers and permission givers. Then both parties practise what some call a pattern of low control, but high accountability. Both have to tolerate the emergence of a more messy church life than is familiar in respectable established churches, as the indigenous churches follow the advice of Roland Allen. He taught that the local community should sort out its own internal discipline issues and so grow in maturity.

Formal marks of being Anglican

These marks include the following: the Declaration of Assent made by a church leader to the historic Christian faith, being in communion with the diocesan bishop, unity within a diversity set by the parameters of the Lambeth Quadrilateral, and the practice of authorized patterns of baptism and communion.

While it is theologically and legally true that these delineate the present understanding of what it is to be Anglican, they are more tangential when it comes to the issue of maturity. None of these confers maturity, they are more about identity. The two are not unconnected. Those who are secure in their identity have foundations that enable them to demonstrate maturity. However, it would be ecumenically ludicrous to claim that only Anglicans can be mature Christians, or that all convinced Anglicans are mature, or only Anglican churches are mature. Equally, it is good that the leaders of a fresh expression of church know the theological and ecclesial framework in which they exist, of which they are part, and which sends them out. This gives a core of the tradition of faith to which they listen in the missionary double listening process.

It is likely that, in seeking to become mature, fresh expressions of church will be on a journey towards a practice of baptism and communion. Here context and intention are most important. If in its mission there have not yet been converts who are ready for baptism, do we really want to say that an expression is not yet Church? Similarly in growing church among some non-churched people, starting patterns of public worship with Communion may be excluding and alienating. However, as people encounter Jesus and learn to make his wishes central, they will read the Gospels. When they encounter the stories of the Last Supper and of the great commission, I would be confident that the Holy Spirit will teach them to embrace these sacramental realities of communal church life. Even then maturity is not automatically conferred by either baptismal or eucharistic practice, as Paul has to remind the Corinthian Christians. As often in the Christian life, it's not what we do, but the spirit in which it is done.

The potential to reproduce

The life cycle of all living things includes the creation of the next generation. In younger human beings the body undergoes changes that indicate this onset of the potential for reproduction and this process is even talked of as part of maturing. In the human world it is thought best that reproduction is deferred until a certain level of maturity is attained, not least because of the physical risks involved and in order to care for the dependent young being raised.

If the Church is more fundamentally organic and relational, than organiza-tional and intuitional, then the dimension of reproduction is another mark of maturing worth noting. *Mission-shaped Church* took such a view and devotes a section of its most theological chapter to the ecclesial equivalent of this reality, even going as far as saying 'This is an essential dimension of any missionary ecclesiology.'[10] It roots within the broad sweep of salvation history the argument for a divine mandate for the Church to be able to reproduce. Within that framework God makes covenants with Adam and Abraham and initiates a mission of multiplication from the few to the many. This emphasis is continued in Christ who tells many parables of reproductive growth from small beginnings. His titles, which include the new Adam, with the Church described as a new creation, underscore this perception. The process of reproduction continues until the return of Christ, when it is deemed complete.

This theological foundation underpins a strand of the previous section, the quality of self-propagation.

It is possible that one gift, to the rest of the Church, from the fresh expressions and church planting fraternity, is the restoration of this dynamic of reproduction. To see it as a normal part of the way in which the Church is intended to grow and as one valid dimension of assessing maturity is a new perspective, to a long-established Church that can think that longevity and unchanging stability are the key marks of maturity. Some care and qualification is needed at this point. There is no argument being made here that churches should irresponsibly proliferate, without respite or thinking through issues of timing and longer sustainability that affect the sending and sent church communities. But equally, to exclude this dynamic is to ignore an obvious challenge from nature. It is to deny some intriguing patterns of salvation history and to undercut a dynamic essential in the creation of fresh expressions.

No single timescale

In nature, different animals come to physical and behavioural maturity over different lengths of time. For example, some larger dogs take two years to settle down. Human beings take far longer. Among some people, who are adult in years, maturity still seems far off. We should expect that fresh expressions will not take a fixed length of time to mature. It will depend on several factors; one is the volume of resources sent to establish a work, but another is the history of a place or culture. In the analogy of farming, mission tasks are described as fields. Some will be fields among the non-churched, where there has been no equivalent of ploughing or sowing – that is, no effective Christian contact, loving service or witness. Beginning church here is inherently a far longer task than where there is connection with a culture in which sustained and appreciated contact with Christian people has occurred. The Church of England has long known its heartlands and wastelands. Growing mature church in both contexts will take different lengths of time.

Constraints preventing maturity

Maturity is not totally in the hands of pioneer ministers. It could be prevented by denial of resources – leaders, team members or finance. One present curse is the three years seed corn syndrome. It is long enough to start but not to sustain. I know of no sustained fresh expressions of church, showing all these marks of maturity, that does not have a full-time leader. If it is argued that this is not necessary, why are leaders almost invariably appointed to old expressions of church?

The opposite error is akin to the well-meaning offer of King Saul's armour to a young David facing Goliath. Burdening fresh expressions with cumbersome structures and organizational commitments, usually in relation to the wider church, is not wise. A similar burden is imposing alien cultural norms on indigenous people. This could include governmental patterns or tight liturgical requirements.[11]

Other constraints observed over the years include church plants being denied permission to reproduce further, though their growth and opportunities warranted it. Equally disturbing is the re-occurring pattern of fresh expressions of church, from a former era, being closed down by incoming incumbents. It connects to the restraints on planted fresh expressions of church being granted legal identity and rights of succession in leadership, although being invited, rightly, to give to parish share. Taxation without representation is not helpful to inculcate interdependence and maturity. If the Church of England ever makes its church plants and fresh expressions into bonsai specimens, it should not complain that they don't mature properly.

Is maturity in all dimensions always possible?

Small-sized church communities like Cells, a youth church, or a midweek congregation of toddlers and their carers, would not find it possible to fulfil all these criteria. The same is true of a significant number of congregations in rural and inner-city areas. The latter may have the legal and historical on their side, but to be self-financing, let alone self-reproducing, when faced with an expensive historic building and the stipend of a full-time leader is beyond them. Perhaps it helps to try and distinguish between maturity, independence and health. There are doubtless some splendid but frail people who are wonderfully mature, but who are utterly dependent on the care of others as they approach dying.

Maturity does not necessarily mean being a healthy adult. If maturity is related to age and stage, then some youthful fresh expressions can be asked to exhibit maturity about their fire, enthusiasm and passion, but it may be unwise to ask for sophistication. On the other hand it may even be that some congregations will be called to be mature about their demise, but it would not then be sense to burden them with expectations of growth.

Maturity is desirable in human beings, but its absence does not destroy their identity as human. So it is probably true that those churches – whether recently or anciently created – that are not mature do not cease to be church. They are marred or unwell churches. However the more flagrant the immaturity, the more they may be seriously flawed. This can lead even to schism, apostasy or extinction.

Maturity is elusive

Jesus' parable of the wheat and the tares (Matthew 13.24-30) shows us a world in which best intentions are mixed with corrupting influences. Furthermore, hopes of separating them to preserve the pure Church are forbidden by his story. Yet in that confusing and competing world a messy process towards maturity occurs. Progress to simple unfettered maturity is unlikely.

At best the Church is a sign of the kingdom. But even the kingdom has a now and not yet quality. Now you see it now you don't. Church in this world will never be more than the kingdom. We should therefore expect church to exhibit a now and not yet quality. Church is itself an incomplete thing. Made of fallen human beings still being transformed, how can it be other than that? Set within the kingdom dynamic it will at best point beyond itself to the God of hope.

We should expect that maturity in all churches, whether fresh or older than that, is an elusive calling. It is to be aimed at but will take a lifetime to pursue. Which one of us is always mature? Why do we have the confession in services every week if maturity is so attainable? Martin Luther, that earthy Christian, spoke of the Church as being a barracks of solders and a hospital of sinners. Let us all be modest about any maturity we think has been achieved.

So the marks explored that could indicate some level of maturity need taking with a pinch of salt. The danger of many of them is that they could be subverted to assess external criteria. To become Pharisaic over maturity would be deceptive. Do we govern ourselves, pay our way and produce lay ministry? Does that alone mean we are a three self church that has arrived at maturity? I doubt it. What of our motives? What of the gap between the calling from God and how we have been able to respond?

Do we hold acts of worship, have community meetings, conduct pieces of mission to the surrounding community and pay the parish share? Does that make us fully holy, one, apostolic and catholic? I doubt it. How are we being transformed in continued encounter with Jesus Christ? How are we being caught up into his life, his values, his self-giving, so that our community radiates his life? Is the mission shaping us or are we still only playing church-shaped mission? What do we really think of those bits of the rest of the Church that think differently from us? I suspect maturity is a long game.

The language of *expressions* of church offers us all some humility in our self-assessment and in our relationships in the wider church. It instantly admits to partial communication of a fuller reality. You see my expression but not yet my soul. Expression language owns up to provisionality. An expression of being church is for here and for now. It is not even perfect at being that. An expression can never be the full story. An expression cannot be the whole church, much less the totality of the Christ. The New Testament writers assert that we are the Body of Christ. No wonder our best attempts are only expressions.

By all means let us work for the maturing of fresh expressions. Let us try to ensure that in the wider Church there is a level playing field about resources to help them with that goal of maturity. But let us also be aware that the criteria for maturity we discover will ask searching questions of all expressions. Maturity was never about putting others down. The path toward maturity will take us all to the edge of our current progress of growing up into Christ.

What does working for maturity mean in practice?

For the pioneers, I suggest working at these values – much like St Paul with his young churches:

- Don't confuse growth, or blessing, with maturity – help the young church work at both tasks.
- Be patient with yourself and the people because instant maturity is impossible. Following Christ is the walk, growing like Christ is the aim.
- Expect a ride with ups and downs and a messy community life. Remember (or discover) what having young children is like.
- It's how the young community recovers from the mistakes made that builds maturity.
- Because what you lead is fresh you will have to learn by trial and error. Squirrel away lessons of good and bad practice and test them with others.

- Find, or form, networks of other leaders who are in the same boat. Email contact is better than none.
- Be clear to whom you are accountable, invite them to see what is happening and genuinely consult with them.

For the permission givers, I suggest the following:

- Treat the leaders in the best way that they are treating their young churches.
- Praise what is achieved and encourage reflection on what still is needed.
- Encourage fresh expressions ministers and churches to meet each other and with you.
- Value their risk taking and energy.
- Encourage longer rhythms of seasons, retreats and recreation.
- Keep the long term sustainability issues before you – they will look after this week's tasks.
- Like a good parent, stand up for them when they are criticized for their youth or vigour.

Discussion questions

How is maturity different from being adult?

What would that look like in a young church?

Consider a particular fresh expression of church. How has it progressed towards maturity when assessed against the marks outlined above?

11

Reconfiguring a diocese towards mission

Ian Cundy

Dioceses and bishops have a vital role in developing a mixed economy Church. Ian Cundy, Bishop of Peterborough, argues on the basis of his own recent research that many dioceses are taking this strategic role seriously. He argues for the integrity of the local parish and also for a major role for deaneries in developing mission and building catholicity and connection.

In his advocacy of contemporary strategies for growth, *Hope for the Church*, and *The Road to Growth* Bob Jackson talks of 'the vital role of the diocese'.[1] He argues that in many areas of church life, 'the unit and instigator of change can only be the diocese ... The way the Church of England is organised, only the diocese can offer the continuity and oversight needed for the long haul in each area'.[2] He also believes that 'if the Church of England wants to be true to its original purpose – to be the church for everyone – it needs to supplement its geographically defined parishes with some relationally defined ones, in which "neighbours" do not live next door to each other but are part of the same people "subgroup"'.[3]

To achieve this dioceses need to start thinking strategically about new patterns of church life; recognizing and training new forms of ministry for rural parishes and developing 'new forms of organization as alternatives to the nightmare of large-number, multi-parish benefices'.

So, how have the dioceses measured up to this challenge? What theological questions might they want to ask in the light of their own strategic thinking? For example, is it right to argue from an agreed sense of the need for the gospel to speak into and within every culture to a new theology of Church, based not on the principle of catholicity – embracing all in each and every place – but on the principle of natural 'relationships'; a Church for the young, for every 'network', a Church of the like-minded? Isn't the point of the parable of the Good Samaritan that my 'neighbour' neither lives next door nor belongs to my 'network'? These questions must be addressed if we are to seize the present opportunity and build the kingdom in our postmodern context.

Current diocesan strategies

Two years ago, I took the opportunity of a sabbatical to study the strategies for mission and ministry that dioceses had developed. Although each diocesan strategy has distinctive features – and different nomenclature – there is sufficient common ground to be able to isolate the significant developments that have taken place in the Church of England's thinking in recent years.

The common themes that have emerged are familiar ground:

- the need to structure the Church to fulfil its God-given mission;
- to develop and encourage the gifts for ministry of God's people;
- to work collaboratively across parochial and denominational boundaries;
- to promote ministry teams;
- to face the challenge of changing resources.

These are all part of the agenda of the Church in each diocese as well as among our ecumenical partners. They stem from both the theological thinking of recent years and the financial and other pressures we face.

Some dioceses, particularly those whose strategies have been published more recently, have been more overtly conscious of the work of others. But whether they have consulted others or not, my own study confirms Gordon Kuhrt's analysis in his symposium, *Ministry Issues*, where he acknowledged 'the surprising degree of common analysis and shared commitment' in diocesan thinking, and identified eight major planks of diocesan strategy.[4]

Gordon Kuhrt also reminds us of further strategic issues that affect the clergy role, many of which were focused in three debates in the General Synod in February 2004. *Mission-shaped Church* indicated some of the creative ways in which the mission of the Church is transcending the parish structure; the McClean Report, *Review of Clergy Terms of Service*,[5] charted the changing context for the employment of the clergy, and suggested a way forward in the light of recent legislation which would give a clear status and appropriate protection to the clergy. With a clear requirement of Ministry Review, and continuing Ministerial Education, it would formalize a widely accepted understanding of the role of the clergy; thirdly, the Toyne Report, *A Measure for Measures*,[6] introduced proposals for replacing the Pastoral and related Measures, with a new Measure for Mission and Ministry. This would intend to simplify the processes of pastoral reorganization and create a legal framework for the initiatives proposed in *Mission-shaped Church*. The outworking of the Toyne report is itself the subject of the final chapter of this book.

These developments create the potential for a radical restructuring of the Church of England. They also present us with a theological challenge about the nature of the Church. The history of Protestantism since the Reformation is bedevilled (and I do not think that is too strong a word) by the fragmentation that results from the development of congregations, and then 'churches' of the like-minded. Loosened from the bonds of episcopal and/or conciliar structure, the churches became fissiparous by nature. So if these modern developments are to remain within the catholic Church as we know it, then clearly lessons have to be learnt and cautions heeded.

What's in a name? From parishes and benefices to localities and 'sustainable units'

Many dioceses have responded to the challenge of becoming a 'mission-shaped' Church by arguing for larger geographical units, though, because PCCs, patrons, and deanery synods have stressed the importance of the 'local' in the sense of the local parish, its church and council they have also stated their intention to continue supporting the parish system where it is seen to be working.

In stating that the parish system should remain the norm, the diocese of Sheffield argued:

> This means priests working with others, both inside the local church congregation and in the wider community, within a defined geographical area:
>
> - It identifies the Church with particular localities, needs and people.
>
> - It incarnates the Church locally, making it available to all, with a visible presence.
>
> - It defines an area of responsibility, crucially that the gospel is for all people in the community and not just the gathered: for

the ordained, it allows freedom in ministry and job satisfaction; for the laity, it encourages the sense of service to everyone in the area where God has placed us.

● It allows for a plurality of churchmanship, tradition, worship and outreach.

● [It is] the preferred arrangement amongst most clergy and laity in the Diocese of Sheffield.[7]

Yet ever since the Paul Report of 1964[8] we have been told that the parish system has broken down, at least in many areas, and needs to be replaced. For example, Bishop Michael Turnbull, then Bishop of Durham, wrote in 2001:

I believe we need to think radically about the parish as we now have it. In many areas the parish hinders mission rather than enhancing it. This suggestion is not abandoning the geographical elements of the present system but changing present perceptions of what a parish is.[9]

He believes that many parishes create low morale, with elderly congregations and discouraged clergy prevented from developing lay ministry and mission-orientated strategies. In contrast, others are strong, reflecting the seven marks of a healthy church, developed by Robert Warren from research in the Durham diocese.[10]

Bishop Michael Turnbull therefore wants to argue for 'localities':

We are a people called to reflect God's nature to the world. And his nature is not hierarchical and distant but relational and inclusive. That becomes a model of being the Church. The marks of such a people are precisely those that Gordon Kuhrt has described – collaborative, waiting on God's grace, and relating to the real social structures in which people operate.

So I suggest we:

1. emphasize the value of *locality* but recognize that for most people this is not the *parish* as we have known it;

2. look to establishing locality ministries rather than current parish ministry.

Locality ministries may include neighbourhood worship but wider learning activities and engagement with the community and church administration would be on the scale of the locality.[11]

While this is a route that many others dioceses have followed, it is not immediately apparent how this pattern is more relational and inclusive, and less hierarchical and distant than a good multi-parish benefice (or a 'minster' model) where there is real collaboration between the constituent parishes, including the sharing of ministerial skills, and a common strategy for mission; particularly where some care has been taken to ensure that the benefice is not arbitrarily formed but has taken account of the social patterns of the area.

Others have argued for a similar pattern from a concept of 'subsidiarity' which, rightly understood, is a 'bottom up' concept. Decisions should be taken in the appropriate 'locality' unless the result has wider implications. Then authority must be given from the locality to a more 'central' body to make the decision for all. 'Delegation' with which it is often confused works the opposite way – the centre delegates decisions to the local. Wherever we locate authority – centrally or dispersed – the intention must be to enable decisions to be made at an appropriate 'level', be it parish, 'locality', deanery or diocese.

Names do matter, of course, and areas of mission or sustainable units of mission carry their own valuable, though value-laden, definition of the unit's purpose. On the other hand the word 'parish', derived from the Greek, *par(a)oikia* – literally 'beyond the household' – is part of our history. It describes both a geographical area and a unit of governance, originally in secular and then in church government. Its continuing significance is described by Archbishop Rowan Williams as 'a relation of *loyalty* between church and society', and it continues to focus the importance of the local, based on a sound theology of 'place'. Such a theology avoids the false dichotomy of contrasting 'maintenance' and 'mission'. You cannot be in mission if you are not there. 'Presence' in a locality (or a network) is a pre-requisite of shaping it in the light of God's kingdom as Robin Gamble argues (see Chapter 7 above).

Given its long history, highlighted by Martyn Percy (in Chapter 1), the desire to keep faith with its principles, and its continued use in secular government, dioceses need seriously to consider whether they are wise to try and introduce a new language, which will only have meaning to the gathered community of the faithful. All agree that parishes need to work more closely together in a way that releases rather than stretches to breaking point the gifts of the ordained and authorized ministers; that they need to develop a way of being in tune with God's mission which relates to the reality of people's situation and networks; and that they need to make some hard decisions about buildings. Much of that can be achieved at the deanery level, if deaneries are empowered by the parishes (subsidiarity) and by the diocese (delegation) to do it. It can be effected, in a sustainable way, by using the present language, provided we do not interpret 'parish' as meaning 'parochialism' with all its defensive strategies for preserving 'our' vicar and our way of doing things.

As Michael Moynagh (see Chapter 8 above) has described, the loyalty to the very local is increasingly eloquent in certain parts of modern society and is a counterweight to government and Church policy which seeks delivery of services through larger units, for example, market towns and 'minster' churches in many rural areas. It is a reminder that human beings need to be 'earthed' and react to the impersonal anonymity of many urban landscapes. Indeed much modern planning of new towns incorporates 'townships' or village-scale developments within the larger unit. At the end of the day community remains an elusive concept and we may give different accounts of where we belong, and whether geography is important in defining our identity.

While these loyalties remain, the Church would be wise to seek an evolutionary development, building on the existing parish/benefice pattern, rather than a revolutionary change of nomenclature as well as structure. To achieve that needs clarity of vision and the patience to take people with you, building bridges of understanding and shared experience.

Still a 'Church for all' – responding to the enquirers' 'touch'

Lying behind the desire to preserve what is best of the parish system is a view of the Church of England, indeed of the Church, that it should be a church for all who wish 'to touch the hem of its garment' to use the phrase developed by the Bishop of Lincoln, John Saxbee. Others see the church as a gathered community of committed believers. The distinction is usually described as 'associational' on the one hand – embracing those who wish to 'join' – and 'communal' on the other – bound up with the life of the neighbourhood. Individual congregations in the Church of England may identify strongly with one or other of these models, though many display features of both. But from its beginnings, and its re-formation in the sixteenth and seventeenth centuries, the Church of England has always sought to be a church for all. What that means has developed from an identity of Church and 'Commonwealth' for many of the Reformers to, in a more diverse community, an understanding of the openness of the Church to all who wish to seek her ministry, and of the need to address the demands of the gospel to the structures and organizations of society.

Paul Avis argues that historically since the Reformation we have moved from a 'Nation-as-Church' model, through one based on 'Episcopal Succession' to a 'Communion-through-baptism' model of self-understanding.[12] Nevertheless, we have retained features of that history: from the first model the Church's mission to all:

> Anglicanism can never be a sect. The Church of England is a territorial church and embraces all within its parishes who do not refuse its ministry, and the role of the laity in church government (including the authority to reform ourselves); and from the second, the importance of remaining in communion with, and giving canonical obedience to one's bishop as the focus of unity.

All diocesan strategies have sought to maintain that commitment to a territorial structure. Indeed, some of the problems that face us most acutely could be said to arise from the desire to maintain that ideal in spite of the pressures of finance and a smaller stipendiary priesthood. How can the structure be effectively developed in the face of the significant shift in the structure of ministry from one in which the role of the clergy is dominant, to one in which pastoral and evangelistic ministry is shared with the 'richer tapestry' of ministry, both lay and ordained?

The burden of *Mission-shaped Church* is that 'being there for all' in modern Britain, also means taking 'networks' seriously. This is leading to a variety of models at the local level – 'cell' churches, church 'plants', 'pub' churches, youth churches and so on. Some of these mission initiatives will tend towards an associational model, and wrestle with difficult questions as they become eucharistic communities wondering how they relate to the other eucharistic communities around. Theologically, the catholicity of the Church means, among other things, that it embraces every race, class, culture, age and social status. Any 'network' expression of the Church must therefore, like every other expression of the Church, be it parish, local congregation, deanery or diocese, retain that sense of belonging to something beyond itself, as George Lings argues, and also help people to appreciate their baptismal and eucharistic involvement with the wider community of the Church. It is partly for this reason that *Mission-shaped Church* and the *Dioceses, Mission and Ministry* legislation stress the role of the bishop in relation to these developments; to remain in communion with one's bishop is a symbolic expression of this catholicity.

The other response to the need to relate to networks and other patterns of society has traditionally been expressed through the role and language of chaplaincy highlighted by Ann Morisy in Chapter 9. Some diocesan strategies (for example, Newcastle) have specifically highlighted the role of chaplains as central to their mission. They rightly remind us that in times of financial strain, we should resist the temptation to cut everything that is not parochial. These ministries can be just as much part of the rationale of the parish system – being there for all – as the geographical model.

If therefore we are to maintain this theological principle in our highly complex society, with its variety of networks and structures, we need to engage in the important but apparently neglected theological discussion of the way in which new patterns of church life fit in with the vision of the catholicity of the Church which transcends these temporary social constructs, without ignoring their reality. We will not wish to do so uncritically but we must not let our familiarity and long experience of one way of 'being there for all' prevent the development of other models. As always we need to live within our culture, as well as living our vocation to be 'counter-cultural' where the kingdom of God requires us to be.

Empowering the deaneries

If the church's task is continuously to re-orientate its life in the light of the mission of God and become an effective Christian presence within the different communities at the parish, or local level, what do we need the deanery, and the diocese to do in order to fulfil that role? And, if either the parishes or the dioceses give the deanery a greater role, does it – as some have suggested – fundamentally alter the nature of the Church? To answer those questions we need to look honestly at the reality on the ground.

Many dioceses already delegate to the deaneries the responsibility for apportioning the parish share, recognizing that not all parishes or even benefices can adequately meet their own costs. Under these strategies dioceses also want to delegate responsibility for (or at least the giving of advice about) developing a strategy for mission, including the deployment of available resources of ministry, the clustering of parishes, the responsibility for decisions about buildings, and the development of new initiatives.

Every diocese has its 'viable' churches. With congregations of 100–150 plus, they are able to raise enough money to look after their buildings, provide the costs of their ministry, lay and ordained, including the costs of housing, pensions, training, through their contributions to the 'parish share' or 'family purse'. Indeed many of the larger churches are contributing to the costs of the ministry in other parts of the diocese. These churches will also have a 'ministry team', which shares with the clergy the task of pastoral leadership; hopefully they will also have a thriving ministry to young people and to the schools in the parish. Such churches are largely (but not exclusively) to be found in city centres, in the suburbs and in the larger market towns.

In rural areas, housing estates and the poorer areas of our larger conurbations, however, it will often be a different story. In some rural benefices, where pastoral reorganization has brought together a sufficient number of smaller parishes, they will be able to cover their costs – but with six or more church buildings to look after, rather than one, they carry a significantly larger financial burden. They will do so, even though their congregations are small in number – though in terms of the proportion of the population who are worshipping members of the church they may be well ahead of any other parish. For example, a hamlet with a population of 40 and a fine medieval church may regularly attract 10–12 local people for worship, more than 25 per cent of the population! They are also able to tap into the affection of the local community for their historic building – and the growing number of 'Friends of St Peter's' and similar organizations has contributed substantially to the good state of repair of many village churches. In others, where the PCC or the incumbent with the 'freehold' has resisted pastoral re-organization, one or two small congregations will not be able to cover the costs of maintaining the priest in his or her small rural cure. As a result, they remain a financial 'receiver' from the other congregations of the diocese. Such 'parochialism' needs to be faced for what it is.

There will always be 'areas of mission' that need financial as well as other support; as a result dioceses will continue to need some means of sharing the costs of mission and ministry – the true purpose of 'parish share'. But the vast bulk of the benefices in the Church must face the challenge of covering their costs, and also make a contribution to the mission of God in the rest of the diocese. There is still a task of education to be done. More parishioners need to grasp the reality that their contribution to parish share is covering the cost of ministry in the parish, as well making a small contribution to the mission of the Church in areas of genuine need. In spite of all the work that has been done over the years, too many people still regard the 'share' as a diocesan 'tax' to finance 'the centre' or resent an apparent subsidy being given to parishes whom they regard as 'failing'. As Bob Jackson records, some dioceses are tackling the issue by asking parishes to meet their own ministry costs rather than making a contribution to the diocesan budget.[13]

That requires some means of deploying ministry 'fairly' to fulfil the mission of the Church, and to avoid wealthy parishes using their resources to fund their own vicar and employ lay workers without regard to the mission of the Church in the neighbouring parish, let alone the rest of the diocese. To achieve this many dioceses have enhanced the role of the deaneries, asking both parishes and the diocesan authorities to empower them to make decisions about deployment, size of 'benefices', or clusters of parishes, and the apportionment of costs amongst the PCCs.

Deaneries could also have a role in integrating new initiatives into the life of the Church of England. If all such initiatives were supported and monitored by the deanery from their outset – rather than remaining the vision and the responsibility of one parish – then the problem of cross-boundary initiatives would be addressed in a context in which all the parishes had a voice, and the initiative would command the active support in prayer and giving of the wider community of the Church. The bishop would then know that he had the support of the deanery in creating a 'mission initiative' and in licensing a priest to focus its worship and lead its mission. He would also be able to draw on the agreed strategy and the local knowledge of the deanery in finding the right way forward when the initiative moves from an experiment in mission to an equal partner with the other worshipping communities in the locality. Doubtless, because we are all human, tensions would still emerge, but if the deanery became a forum for their resolution – and was accepted as such by the clergy and congregations – before any scheme was drawn up, then much time-wasting disagreements could be avoided.

If deaneries are of reasonable size and relate to clear social boundaries – for example, boundaries of civil administrations; a focal market town and its 'satellites' – then the following scenario should be workable:

- Each deanery would develop *a mission plan* with the support of the parishes; it would look at the resources needed to develop new initiatives, such as church plants in new estates; outreach to the young people of the area; support for the Church and other schools; chaplaincy to institutions, as well as the existing parochial appointments.

- In developing its mission plan the deanery would have *a serious engagement with its ecumenical partners*, especially, in the light of the Anglican–Methodist Covenant, with the superintendent minister of the

Methodist circuit (whose chapels may lie within a similar boundary), so that, wherever possible, new initiatives could be fully ecumenical and resources could be deployed collaboratively, not competitively.

● The deanery would be responsible for developing *a strategy for the deployment of ministry* – both lay and ordained, stipendiary and non-stipendiary – in the light of the anticipated deployment of stipendiary priests (using a 'Sheffield'-type formula) agreed with the diocesan synod, for the next five-year period. Part of that strategy might well be the encouragement of specific vocations to these ministries to provide adequate leadership for the future.

● They would recommend to the Pastoral Committee how *existing parishes/ benefices could be brought together in viable units*, both for effectiveness in mission, and financial sustainability; with the agreement of the committee they would set achievable targets to bring these groupings into existence.

● They would encourage *new initiatives – church plants, fresh expressions, network evangelism – to be accountable to the deanery* through the chapter (or ministers fraternal) who share responsibility with the bishop and the diocesan synod for deploying resources of finance and ministry.

● They would develop *a financial strategy* to enable each grouping to raise sufficient money to support the costs of mission and ministry in the whole deanery (including the costs of Church schools), and make a small contribution to the diocese to cover the cost of diocesan administration and the diocesan mission fund, from which specific grants could be made for new mission initiatives in the deaneries.

Many current strategies move in this direction. In doing so, they are moving some decisions nearer to the parishes, as well as asking the parishes to recognize the value of sharing resources and needs more widely. This approach was advocated in 1983 by John Tiller in his report (though few, if any, have followed his division between 'diocesan' and 'local' priests).[14] As he explained at the time such a strategy builds on processes and patterns already in existence, rather than creates a totally new structure.

But whether or not larger groupings embrace the whole deanery, do these developments represent 'a significant change in our understanding of the church' and transform the Church of England into 'an "associational church" ... distancing the church from the life of the local community'?

In one regard the 'visibility' of the Church in the local community may be diminished. With fewer stipendiary clergy 'on the ground' – rather like local policemen or doctors – they cannot be community figures to an increasing number of communities. Particularly where a Minster model with the clergy living in the central town, or a clustering of multi-parish benefices, is developed there is this potential danger. We must also acknowledge the crucial role of the ordained and lay ministers in encouraging growth, as Bob Jackson argues.[15] But if the parish still remains the basic unit, the Church is still a Church for all, and with the careful deployment of non-stipendiary and ordained local ministry as well as Readers, there can still be a 'pastoral focus' in each community, and possibly in the key 'networks'. The real change in ecclesiology is one to which we have given lip-service over the years and is now becoming a reality – the church is not 'the clergy' but the Body of Christ, relational and organic, in which the gifts of God's people are nurtured and used. An effective Christian presence needs the leadership provided by a ministry team, *and* the representative ministry of an ordained person. Where the ministry is shared, he or she can be freed to be the truly representative person they were ordained to be; others can be the focus of Christian presence in each community.

There is therefore no need for the Church to move in a more 'associational' direction under these strategies, unless the local church tries to make their vicar do and be everything that the Church should represent in the local community. Indeed it is arguable that the way the Church had developed in the nineteenth and early twentieth century has hampered the sharing of resources across parochial boundaries with the result that the sense of partnership and collaboration which is of the essence of the Church has become obscured, or restricted to work within, and not between, congregations. To work with larger units, while retaining the importance of the 'local' for the mission of the Church is not only practically sensible, but theologically sound.

Because deanery synods do not have the same legal functions as PCCs and diocesan synods they have always had considerable freedom in setting their agendas. With good leadership, many have already seen their role as supporting the mission of the parishes, and developing a sense of vision for the whole deanery to which the parishes have contributed. This enhanced role would enable them to develop that function and give the synod some 'teeth' – an authority to coordinate and focus the purpose and mission of the Church in and to the community, to deliver with diocesan help the training and supportive role of specialist advisers and trainers and to bring policy and finance together at a more local level than the diocese.

Some have suggested that such a strategy is 'managing decline' rather than promoting mission. As one priest recently said to me of his diocese's policy of 'clustering' parishes, 'it is dishonest to present it as a strategy for mission, when we all know it is forced upon us by the declining number of priests'. The *Growing Healthy Churches* material presents a different picture. Where churches are outward looking – welcoming, building good relationships, reaching out to the community, recognizing and challenging injustice, nurturing faith in Christ – all centred in worship and intercession on behalf of the community, they continue to be effective communities of mission.

Although we certainly have fewer stipendiary priests, we are not seeing a decline in authorized ministry, but a significant burgeoning of the recognition and acknowledgement of the gifts of the lay people, or rather the 'non-ordained', within the congregation. There is also a significant increase in non-stipendiary priests and ordained local ministers. This burgeoning of ministry requires bishops to give a 'variety of permissions' and to help the parishes and the diocese embrace *the re-orientation* of what we are doing in the light of the *mission of God.*

It is the role of the bishop and his staff who have the 'over-sight' of the diocese and see the big picture, to ask how the mission of the Church is to be maintained in the present circumstances and with the resources available. The mission of God is central to its purpose and must flow organically from its worship. As a bishop I feel committed to the task, with the help of my colleagues, of maintaining and developing an effective, outward-looking, worshipping Christian presence in every community throughout the diocese, and developing such an effective presence in each new development and network. It is a demanding task, but that is where our focus should be.

The role of the bishop

Leadership in Anglican polity has personal as well as collegial and communal dimensions. In developing any strategy for the diocese, as *Mission-shaped Church* indicated, the attitude of the bishop is crucial. The bishop focuses the life and mission of the Church in the diocese, and of the wider Church to the diocese. As the person who has the oversight of the diocese, he is uniquely placed to 'see over' the whole and to enable strategic thinking to take place at every level, working closely with representatives of the whole people of God in the diocese. The phrase 'the bishop in synod' expresses a view of the governance of the Church, which is neither hierarchical nor monarchical and authoritarian. Rather, it speaks of an authority exercised in relationship, communally with the people of God, collegially with episcopal colleagues.

Although the Church is not a parliamentary democracy – in spite of the way in which the media views the General Synod – episcopal authority is exercised in collaboration with his senior colleagues and as a focus of the mind of the People of God, expressed by 'walking together' in synodical discussion.

The role of the bishop as a leader in mission is expressed both by personal example, and also by working to ensure that the structure and strategy of the diocese is shaped by the mission of God for his Church. The strategy must support the mission of the parishes and the deaneries as they seek to carry out their God-given task. Part of the role of leadership is to think systemically, and many have reflected with profit on Peter Senge's threefold role for servant leaders: 'designers' who give their attention to the governing ideas in an organization; 'teachers' who articulate the tension between vision and current reality; and 'stewards' who embody the desire to serve.[16]

As the person with the authority to ordain, and to license, the bishop has a particular responsibility for the ministry, both lay and ordained, and its deployment. The sharing of decisions in this area with the deaneries as well as the senior staff and the Pastoral Committee, does not remove his ultimate responsibility for deployment; for ensuring that the strength of the Church in some areas is not at the expense of others; and that adequate provision is made for the mission to new developments and extra-parochial institutions.

His active participation in the life of 'fresh expressions' of being Church, as well as the involvement of the deanery, may provide the beginning of an answer to the expressed need to teach and embody the catholicity of the Church in appropriate models. As Paul Bayes states in his (confusingly titled) Grove Booklet, *Mission-shaped Church*: 'Episcopal church order is relational – episcopal Christians relate to one another in communion with and in relation with their bishop. This does not mean we have to agree with him, still less that he has to agree with us. But we define our identity within the Christian family in terms of relationship, and within the episcopal family in terms of *that* relationship.'[17]

In practice much of modern culture with its emphasis on 'doing things my way' and seeking a spirituality that 'works for me' runs counter to this view. The bishop and his colleagues with whom he shares some episcopal functions (archdeacons, rural deans, specialist ministers) must work hard to challenge this high degree of individualism and, with the support of the local priest both teach and embody a relational view of the Church – recognizing that it is 'counter-cultural' in many contexts.

A further complication and opportunity is provided by the commitments that many Church leaders have made through local 'Covenants'. These state that in developing the mission of the Church to new housing estates and other new developments, the Church leaders resolve to work ecumenically wherever possible and appropriate. In such circumstances the creation of a Local Ecumenical Partnership means that the task of *episcope* of the congregation is shared with other Church leaders, usually through the 'sponsoring body' – the intermediate or county ecumenical agency – even where the responsibility for the minister(s) remains with one or more of the individual leaders. This remains a cumbersome, and somewhat bureaucratic, structure of oversight, which does not fit easily with the need for mission initiatives to travel light and be quickly responsive to changes in the local situation. We need a better structure and a willingness to trust each other so that one person can oversee work on behalf of all the partners in the venture.

In this context it is unfortunate that the proposals for an 'ecumenical bishop' in South Wales and Swindon have not, so far, been successfully implemented. Covenants are to be welcomed, but without some proposals along these lines, they do create an extra layer of bureaucracy, which is often resented in our more charismatic and person-focused world.

Questions of governance

Finally, many dioceses have taken the opportunity to review their central structures, both in terms of personnel – often creating an additional member of the training team – and also their pattern of boards and councils. If the diocese is to be re-focussed for mission then the structures that support the work of its officers need to share that focus.

Following the Turnbull report,[18] dioceses, as well as the General Synod have tried to set up structures which bring together policy and finance. In many cases this has led to a clearer definition of the responsibility of the Bishop's Council and diocesan synod.

This is reflected in the development of strategies for ministry, which take into account both the available human resources and the financial position of the diocese. By devolving strategic decisions to the deaneries, they make the local Church aware of the financial realities of their situation and establish a closer connection between the money they raise for the parish share and the remuneration of the costs of ministry in the deanery.

But there are important functions, which the diocese must not abandon. Indeed, on the principle of subsidiarity, there are functions, which the deaneries must give to the diocese with its wider perspective. The officers and the councils of the diocese can see the full picture and create a budget for the work of the whole. They will do so in the light of their assessment of the ability of the parishes to fund the cost of their own ministry and to contribute to the ministries from which they all benefit (from archdeacons to specialist ministers) and to those parts of the mission of the diocese that are paid centrally, for example, chaplaincies (where they are not covered by the institution); schools that may serve more than one deanery; and new initiatives in mission and church planting where seed-corn money is necessary until the deanery can take on the responsibility for funding the work.

The diocese also needs to indicate how the available (and affordable) numbers of stipendiary clergy are to be deployed, either by specifically allocating the projected numbers to the deaneries, or by providing clear guidelines to which the deaneries must work if the diocesan budget, and the target figures for clergy deployment are to be met. Clear figures about the costs of supporting stipendiary, house-for-duty, and non-stipendiary clergy need to be given. No one comes totally 'free', and the costs of housing (for house for duty priests) and training apply to all ordained and accredited lay ministries.

Bob Jackson advocates a more radical restructuring of the diocesan budget, where the parishes become responsible for the cost of their own ministers – 'relying on the generosity of Christian giving freely entered into through personal relationships'.[19] Some dioceses – for example, Chester and Lichfield – have begun to move in this direction. Whatever the system, experience suggests that where the object is clear and the need established, people will give and give sacrificially. As in other areas they need to catch the vision and feel that they have played their part in its development.

Faced with the potential need to develop a mission to new housing estates and to finance new initiatives in mission, many dioceses have set up a mission fund. The money that the Church Commissioners were able to set aside in 2002 and subsequent years to support initiatives in the dioceses has boosted such funds, and in some cases led to their establishment.

The diocese of Oxford was not alone in deciding that its function should be to create 'strategic directions' for the deaneries and parishes to follow, rather than creating a blueprint for the whole diocese. Others have put more flesh on the bones of the skeleton, to change the metaphor, but have deliberately left the precise details to the local churches to work out.

No diocese has yet addressed the need to reform our synodical processes, where the sense of the bishop in synod listening to what is said and articulating the vision which under the Holy Spirit he senses is emerging (for example, in the Newcastle Mission Statement) is too often lost under formal and procedural motions, which are exploited by the experienced and often confuse the novice. If the Church is to be a 'learning organization' where all are contributing to the process of the organization's learning, it must have the courage to abandon Parliamentary procedures where they are not assisting the process and create the trust to allow bishops to fulfil their role. They in turn must develop better structures of listening, so that they can indeed articulate and share the God-given vision they have discerned.

Conclusion

Anyone who has had the privilege of sharing in the thinking of the dioceses cannot but be impressed with the quality of thought and hard work which has gone into the production of these documents. Certainly there is ample evidence that Bob Jackson's challenge has not gone unheeded. Many dioceses are seeking to think strategically about mission and the shape of a Church which can be said to be 'mission-shaped'. His conclusion, in advocating 'healthy dioceses' that

> a diocese is far more than just an administrative body needed to keep the parish system ticking over. It can hold the key to the future of the Church of England in its locality. By being proactive, by joining up its policies around a coherent aim, by giving strategic impetus to every local church, by all the ways in which it can itself model the marks of the healthy community of faith and help to multiply new and healthy expressions of local church life, the diocese can ensure that the Church grows rather than declines in the twenty-first century.[20]

is reflected in the careful way these strategies have been developed and promoted.

Much of my study would endorse that conclusion, but we must avoid the danger of forging too easy a linkage between 'health' and 'growth'. In spite of all his advocacy of the work of Robert Warren and his emphasis on a 'healthy', rather than a 'successful', diocese there is an un-resolved tension in *Hope for the Church* and *The Road to Growth*. Ultimately they suggest that the final measure of a healthy church is its ability to grow quantitatively, rather than the more qualitative and nuanced septet of 'marks of a healthy church' advocated by Robert Warren.[21] Of course, growth is part of the total picture, but not the sole criterion. It is a sad reflection on the Church's history that numerical strength does not always lead to effectiveness in mission, in transforming the world according to the mind of God.

While dioceses have taken up the challenge of thinking strategically, they recognize that there are important questions still to be faced – particularly about the way in which we seek to be true to our vision of a Church that is one, holy, catholic and apostolic. To integrate fresh expressions into a truly 'catholic' structure is not easy. However, if we can learn the lessons of the past and ensure that this new energy and enthusiasm is genuinely complementary to the strengths of the system we have inherited then we can reverse the apparent decline of the last few years, and develop effective strategies for mission and health. At the end of the day, merely 'managing decline' is in nobody's interests and does not reflect the life of God who calls us to his mission.

The common strands that have emerged speak of a Church that is seeking to be true to the nature of God revealed in Jesus and in the life of the Church down the centuries. There is not only creative thinking, there is vibrant life. While some of the overall statistics may be disturbing, the evidence from churches that are growing, as Robert Warren and others have identified, suggests that where people have caught the vision of what it means to develop a welcoming, outward-looking and socially aware community there is a burgeoning of new life. In creating that community they will be drawing on the gifts that God has generously given to his Church. It is his mission to which we are called; his generous gifts that enable us to fulfil it.

12

Legal matters – what you need to know

John Rees

The development of the mixed economy church needs to be supported by wider changes in our legal structures. John Rees has been closely involved in the development of new legal frameworks as Registrar of the Province of Canterbury and of the Diocese of Oxford. He is currently a member of the commission chaired by the Bishop of Exeter charged with developing the new Dioceses, Mission and Ministry Measure.

'You can't . . . it's against the law!'

That is a response that may have stifled many imaginative initiatives in the Church of England. Perhaps it needn't have done so. The primary obstacles were personal and cultural. As far as the law was concerned, many of the mechanisms for change were there, but the processes were elaborate and not widely understood. It may be understandable that after the major legislative changes of the 1950s and 1960s,[1] the Church of England's General Synod left the detail of pastoral provision in the hands of the small number of *cognoscenti* to whom it had entrusted the task – pastoral secretaries, pastoral committees, and the Church Commissioners. Not all of them were alert to the creative possibilities open to them in the legislative tools they had.[2]

Meanwhile, exciting developments *were* taking place in the life of the Church, mainly around the fringes of its institutions: In the 1970s Christian rock bands were bringing young people together for worship, teaching and evangelism; in the 1980s multi-parish youth fellowships were springing up across deaneries and beyond; in the 1990s cross-boundary church plants were taking root. All had a frisson of illegality about them – which may have been part of their attraction to some of those who were taking part! But it all reinforced the sense that the Church of England was more concerned to maintain its inherited structures than to meet the changing needs of Christian mission in a rapidly changing culture.

That is not to say that the Church's institutional leadership was unaware of what was going on. By the late 1980s, there were profound concerns about the national Church's failure to communicate its message to the nation. A decade later reports and studies proliferated, courses like *Alpha* and *Emmaus* reported burgeoning interest among people who had forgotten what Christian faith was about, or who had never encountered it at all; and the Internet was providing evidence of humanity's profound, and sometimes obsessive, thirst for religion in all its bizarre variety.

A particularly interesting diagnosis emerged from an assessment of the Decade of Evangelism in 1999.[3] In *Setting the Agenda Beyond 2000*,[4] the Church of England's Board of Mission had asked 'What is the Church?', and had responded in terms of 'living in dispersed as well as gathered mode (Monday to Saturday as well as Sunday)' and 'cell mode (geographical, network, community, work-based) as well as congregational and celebration modes'.[5] In part at least, this is the diagnosis that has informed those who, over the last five years, have worked to loosen up the legal structures of pastoral provision for the Church of England.

A Measure for Measures

In 2000 the Archbishops' Council commissioned one of its members, Professor Peter Toyne, to chair a review of the operation of the Dioceses Measure 1978 and the Pastoral Measure 1983. Those legislative Measures between them encapsulate most of the law affecting diocesan boundaries, benefice and parish boundaries, team ministries, suspension of patronage rights, and redeployment of church buildings no longer needed for public worship. The Pastoral Measure is the largest single piece of Church legislation, running to some 130 pages,[6] and the project as a whole was on such a scale that it had to be allocated to no less than three working parties, each reporting to a single main committee. It was the most extensive review of legislation since the General Synod came into existence in 1970.

The Commission's Report *A Measure for Measures*[7] was published in 2004. It made 65 recommendations, for simplifying procedures for change, reducing levels of bureaucracy and providing new approaches to structuring evangelistic enterprise. Above all, it urged that the whole business of pastoral provisions could be shaped by the Church's call to mission. Almost simultaneously another report was published, *Mission-shaped Church.*[8] This report had been produced by the Bishop of Maidstone's working party, on behalf of the Church of England Mission and Public Affairs Council. Both reports emphasize the need for flexibility and responsiveness to 'new ways of being church'.

From the report to legislation

The adoption of most of the recommendations in *A Measure for Measures* was followed by intense drafting work by a steering committee appointed by the General Synod, under the chairmanship of the Bishop of Exeter; and its first draft of a new Dioceses, Pastoral and Mission Measure was endorsed by the first meeting of the newly elected General Synod in November 2005. The next legislative steps will take two years or so to complete, but new arrangements reflecting the emphases of *A Measure for Measures* and *Mission-shaped Church* should be fully in place and operational by the latter part of the five-year life of this General Synod.

What does the new measure do?

Housekeeping functions

The new Measure[9] performs a number of 'housekeeping' functions. It lightens the load of consultation that has to be undertaken in connection with sub-division of benefices and parishes, and puts more of the day-to-day planning and strategy into the hands of those involved at diocesan level (leaving the Church Commissioners with an essentially advisory and appellate function). At the same time, it strengthens the role of the national Dioceses Commission, so that it can initiate a review of diocesan structures without having to depend upon dioceses themselves to do so. Other provisions in the draft Measure simplify the process for closure of church buildings for public worship and/or alternative use for a range of purposes, redevelopment or disposal. The entire Measure is cast in terms of the Church's wider mission.[10]

Mission initiatives

For our purposes, however, the most important proposal relates to 'mission initiatives'.[11] These are projects which may be proposed by the bishop himself, or initiated by other persons or groups, and endorsed by the bishop. The criterion for such endorsement is deliberately broad, encompassing any project which 'would be likely, through fostering or developing a form of Christian community, to promote or further the mission of the Church or any aspect of it'.[12] So it should embrace many of the network church projects that have emerged in recent years, to the extent that they wish to develop identity separate from the parish church which (in most cases) originally sponsored them.

The bishop's endorsement would take the form of a bishop's mission order, which would be made only after ecumenical consultation with other churches, and with interested individuals or groups, as well as with the consent of the Pastoral Committee of the diocese.[13]

The order would specify the role of the leader or leaders of the initiative,[14] but most importantly, the order could contain provisions which would override the 'exclusive cure of souls' enjoyed by Anglican clergy as incumbents or priests-in-charge for generations. This is a major change, which may yet prove highly controversial when it goes to the General Synod for detailed legislative approval. It is carefully hedged around with qualifying provisions, which require bishops to consult clergy whose ministry may be affected, and whole Houses of Clergy in some deaneries or dioceses, where more than one parish, deanery or diocese is affected.[15] Particular care is taken to respect the conscientious concerns of those who cannot accept the validity of women's ordained ministry;[16] and much of the detail as to operation of the orders and mission initiatives is to be spelled out in a code of practice that will be issued by the House of Bishops once the legislation is in an advanced stage of preparation.[17]

The mission initiative will come under a new form of delegated oversight, mediated through a 'Visitor'.[18] The Visitor's role is to oversee, advise, encourage and 'so far as practicable, provide support' for the Initiative; conversely, the leaders of the Initiative are to consult the Visitor regularly about 'general direction and development' of the project, and to provide information to assist the Visitor. There is a particular emphasis on financial accountability,[19] but the underlying purpose of the Visitor's role is to foster linkage between the bishop (as the 'chief pastor' and 'principal minister' in the diocese[20]) and the Initiative authorized by his order. On the face of it, this looks like a role for an archdeacon, but the legislation is deliberately couched in broad terms, and there is no legal reason why the Visitor should not be a lay person.

At the end of the five-year term authorized by the order, the Visitor is to prepare and submit a report to the bishop. The bishop may then renew the order for a further fixed term of up to five years, if he considers that it is right to do so; but there is an expectation built into the legislation that at either this point, after five years, or after an extended period of authorization of up to eighteen months, 'arrangements [may] be made for the mission initiative or its objectives to be continued by other means'.[21] If the term is extended for a full further five-year term, then it may at the end of that extended period be authorized to remain in operation for an indefinite period into the future, but only if the bishop considers that 'there are no other suitable means by which the mission initiative or its objectives can be achieved'.[22]

It seems fairly clear from these provisions, and from the Synod's decision not to revisit the Extra-Parochial Ministry Measure 1967 or the other legal arrangements which currently underpin this kind of mission enterprise, that these mission initiatives are intended to be provisional, flexible and 'lightweight', in answer to the requests that have been made in recent years for more responsive ways of 'proclaiming the word of God and rightly and duly administering the sacraments' in a culture characterized by rapid change and unpredictable patterns of association. Alongside these 'new ways of being church', the legislation very deliberately preserves the familiar patterns of pastoral provision both through parishes and benefices (albeit patterns which in future will be more readily adaptable), and through the provision of non-parish-based ministry which have been tried and tested for forty years or more.

What can already be done?

Since these more familiar provisions are likely to have continuing importance, it may be valuable to remind ourselves what can already be done through creative use of the Extra-Parochial Ministry Measure 1967,[23] and by the development of 'Conventional Districts' under the *Church Representation Rules.*[24]

Chaplaincy ministries

The 1967 Extra-Parochial Ministry Measure was intended to provide a legal structure for ministry by chaplains and other clergy in universities, colleges, schools and other public and charitable institutions[25] without impinging on the ministry of those clergy in whose parishes the institutions are situated. This was another example of the incursion we noted earlier into the 'exclusive cure of souls' entrusted by the bishop to an incumbent or priest-in-charge on their institution or licensing.[26]

Over many years, the ministry of such chaplains and other clergy has been widely appreciated in the institutions in which they have worked, and there is considerable scope within the 1967 legislation for clergy to be licensed to minister to networks of members associated with charitable bodies of one kind or another.[27] This is a provision which could be widely adapted to suit a range of Christian community networks, provided they have charitable status (which most will need for other reasons) and a geographical base from which to operate. The main limitation on the usefulness of this approach is that it does not allow for lay members to become involved as regular members of deanery synods or wider synodical structures.

Conventional districts

'Conventional districts' have had a mixed reception over many years, and unfortunately were regarded with some distain during much of the period in which creative thought has been taking place about 'new ways of being church' in the last decade or so. The reason they have been regarded as unattractive is because their continued existence depends upon the continuing consent of successive incumbents; but in current conditions, the likelihood of such consent being withdrawn by an incoming incumbent is vanishingly small. It is almost unthinkable that a patron would be allowed to appoint as incumbent a priest who would seek to close down a flourishing district church within his or her benefice.

A worked example

In view of comments that have been published about conventional districts, however, it may be worth giving an example of a successful conventional district structure that has been established in recent years. In the diocese of Oxford, major residential development on the outskirts of an outlying town brought into the area significant numbers of Oxford-based workers, a number of whom worshipped at evangelical parishes in the centre of the city of Oxford – twelve miles or so away in a different deanery and a different episcopal area. Some from these evangelical parishes found the Anglo-Catholic style of the parish church in their local town difficult to adopt for themselves; and conversely the priest and people in that parish church did not have the resources to develop the new church base that would be needed to minister to the new population in the rapidly developing part of their parish. After careful negotiation between the incumbents of the parishes concerned, with their PCCs, and also strategic intervention by the Area Bishop at key stages, a new conventional district emerged in 2003.

By way of legal reassurance to those who were putting significant funds into the hands of the new PCC in the conventional district, it was provided that in the event of dissolution, any property or funds belonging to the district PCC would be redistributed only as directed by the Bishop, and not automatically to the PCC of the 'parent' parish in the town. In due course, it is expected that this conventional district will become an entirely separate parish, but even without that step being taken, it is entitled under the Church Representation Rules to have its own Parochial Church Council, and to be fully a part of the deanery in which it is situated. Inevitably, the project has had its ups and downs, but the story is told here to emphasize the continuing usefulness of the concept of the 'conventional district', which may well be one of the ways in which the new mission initiatives may continue to develop after their initial authorization, but before gaining separate existence as part of the more familiar parochial structures.

And finally . . . the limitations of legal review

This chapter is written from a legal perspective. It is intended to show both that the Church's law is in process of adaptation to meet new cultural needs, and that it already has significant, if not widely known, resources for meeting mission needs. However, it would be wrong to imagine that modifying legal structures will usher in the kingdom of God. The role of law is severely limited. At best, it can only buttress structures that assist the work of the kingdom, and provide means for removing obstacles to its advancement or, to change the metaphor, the law's function is to provide a skeleton, upon which a healthy body can develop flesh and sinew.

New patterns of pastoral relationship are emerging fast at the present time, crossing cultural, racial and national boundaries as well as the simple geographical boundaries with which this chapter has been primarily concerned. An area not touched on in this essay is the development of 'virtual' electronic forms of Christian community, as through the 'i-church' in the diocese of Oxford with which the writer has been closely involved. This has been established legally as a separate charitable company, modelled on the pattern of organization of a monastic order and with its members following the Benedictine Rule. It is not entirely obvious whether it would fit into the (still) geographically-based provisions of the new Measure, as it has members, pastoral groups, and group leaders all over the world.[28]

Nevertheless, the new Measure reflects the Church of England's awareness that new initiatives are to be welcomed and 'owned' and need not be objects of suspicion or threat. Christ spoke of the need for new wine to be put into new wine skins (Matthew 9.17), but he also said that the wise teacher was the one who brought out treasures both new and old (Matthew 13.52). It is to be hoped that the new Measure will do justice both to healthy patterns we have inherited from the past, and to the healthy new growth which is emerging in the present and which will emerge in the future. Against such, as St Paul might have said, there should be no law (Galatians 5.23).

Conclusion

Steven Croft

Unity and diversity in a mission-shaped Church: a suggestion

The essays in this book survey and explore the different ways in which the Church of England is seeking to develop its life in the coming decades in a period of continuing cultural change. Underlying all this is the conviction that in the present climate we need to cherish and encourage a mixed economy: the flourishing of many different fresh expressions of church alongside and as part of more traditional parishes.

In the last year and a half I have visited almost every diocese in the Church of England. I have spoken with all kinds of people of the need for this mixed economy to develop. Without exception, and across traditions, there has been a general acceptance that this kind of movement is happening already (to a greater or lesser degree in different places); that it needs to be encouraged; that together we discern God's call to begin to move in these directions.

There are, of course, many practical questions around how we move forward and continue to engage with God's mission in these diverse ways. But there has been one common and over-riding theological question, which I have been asked in almost every context: How will all of this hold together? We see the need for diversity in mission at local level, across a large town or city and across the nation. But the Church is also called to be one. How do we preserve and build unity and coherence across the Church of England while also seeking to encourage this mixed economy in every place?

Since the Reformation, on the surface at least, the unity of the Church of England has been maintained and preserved by holding to uniformity, and particularly uniformity in public worship. That uniformity has been gradually eroding over the last 150 years in an accelerating process both in local use of liturgical texts and in the different phases of liturgical revision. Even 20 years ago, however, it was possible to identify a common similarity in patterns and styles of worship. If this process of erosion continues and accelerates further, then how are we to hold together as one Church? Is there not a danger that the different groups or traditions will have less and less in common and, in the end, find that we pull apart? Where is the common core? What binds us together?

In this concluding reflection, I want to offer a suggestion as to how and where we are discovering our unity even as we become a more diverse Church. It is only a suggestion, and it is a provisional answer. I have reached it in stages as I have tried to answer the question as it has arisen in diocesan synods and gatherings of pioneers, in theological colleges and senior staff meetings. It is, however, a suggestion based as much upon observation and listening ('How *is* all this holding together?') as on prescription ('How can we help build unity within diversity in mission?'). This is because, on the whole, the Church of England is not pulling apart on questions of mission – it is increasingly a commitment to a common mission that holds us together.

This is an answer that I have reached by stages and remains work in progress. Stage 1 was being invited to address the quinquennial conference of the Liturgical Commission in 2005. The overall theme of the conference was liturgy and mission and I was invited to give a plenary address on fresh expressions of church and worship.

My primary observation on worship and fresh expressions of church was that worship is evolving in different ways in different places through an interaction between the Christian tradition on the one hand and the local community and context on the other. That insight was eventually taken up and captured in the final part of definition of fresh expressions of church published in May 2006:

A fresh expression is a form of church for our changing culture established primarily for the benefit of people who are not yet members of any church.

- It will come into being through principles of listening, service, incarnational mission and making disciples.

- It will have the potential to become a mature expression of church shaped by the gospel and the enduring marks of the Church and for its cultural context.

This, of course, raises the question of unity in a Church in which liturgy has historically played such a major role in Christian formation and the transmission of faith from one generation to the next.

My reflection to the liturgical conference was that we are already a very diverse church in terms of its worship. When the Church of England looks in the mirror we only ever see part of our own reflection. Part of this immensely diverse and creative institution is always just out of sight. No one person can actually comprehend, appreciate or understand the whole of this life and diversity.

In terms of our liturgical development over the last 50 years, we have witnessed a shift from unity established through common liturgical *texts* to unity established through common liturgical *shapes*. As Anglicans, we no longer use exactly the same words as we worship together but there remains a recognizable shape to *Common Worship* with varied use of texts.

We are now, I sense, in the midst of a further shift from common shape to common *values* in our worship (and by extension) in our common life. It is, I believe, in the articulation and shaping of common Anglican *values* that we will find, preserve and deepen our unity as the Church of England.

As far as I could tell, the liturgical conference was able to recognize the shift from text to shape to values. I was particularly struck by one conversation after the presentation with a member of the Anglican Communion's Liturgical Commission. Liturgical renewal across the communion, he told me, had passed through a very similar stage of development. Worship in different continents needed to be shaped by the dialogue between a common tradition and a variety of cultural contexts. What would hold us together as a communion was the articulation of common values.

Stage 2 of the journey was, of course, to begin to ask the question: How do we define and describe those values which can be held by every part of the Church of England, which can shape our worship and common life and which can preserve and engender unity in the coming years?

Mission-shaped Church provides some clues and pointers towards an answer to this question but in itself does not provide a full articulation of what might form a common Anglican identity or values for the mixed economy. The five values of a missionary church expounded by Graham Cray still do not give us the building blocks to answer the questions about Anglican unity and ecclesiology (and are not designed to do this). It is immensely important to take our ecclesiology back to first principles, as Rowan Williams does in his chapter on building blocks. However, we are still some way from the question of what holds us together as Anglicans. I therefore began a search for concise and comprehensive statements of Anglican ecclesiology which have some authority in our tradition and which can be carried forward into the shaping of fresh expressions of church.

I also began, very tentatively, to outline a short list of values that might be the shaping values of Anglicanism in the twenty-first century. At first the dialogue was in my head and with colleagues. Then I aired the list in somewhat vague terms in answer to the questions about unity: something about Scripture and sacrament; something about tradition; something about ministry; something about mission to the whole of our society and the whole world. Another penny-dropping moment happened after a presentation in May. 'What you've just described,' said one listener, 'sounds like the Chicago Lambeth Quadrilateral with the addition of the five marks of mission.'

Once again, the situation of the Anglican Communion seemed an excellent parallel for the dilemmas now facing the Church of England. The Communion has lived since its inception with exactly the question of unity in essence but diversity in mission. The Anglican Church worldwide has been shaped by a variety of mission contexts but in dialogue with the historic faith transmitted and preserved through the distinctively Anglican understanding. The key to the preservation of unity in the midst of diversity has been a set of common values which were first articulated and owned in 1888 and which have been the shaping values of the communion to the present day.

Is there a possibility that the capturing and distilling of the values of Anglicanism in the nineteenth century for the Communion might serve us well in articulating and transmitting common values for the Church of England in the twenty-first century? For myself, I think this may be the case and that these particular values might well form an important key to a Church shaped by mission but true to its particular inheritance:

1. a commitment to Scripture;

2. a commitment to the dominical sacraments of baptism and Eucharist;

3. a commitment to listening to the whole of Christian tradition and seeing that tradition expressed in the historic creeds;

4. a commitment to the ministry and mission of the whole people of God and to the ordering of ministry through the threefold order of deacons, priests and bishops;

5.   a commitment to the mission of God to the whole of creation and to the whole of our society as defined and described in the Anglican Communion's five marks of mission.[1]

The worldwide developments in the churches' understanding of the ministry of the whole people of God, owned and affirmed by the Anglican Communion, have informed the development of point 4. The renewal throughout the Church of our understanding of mission and the commitment made by the Communion to the marks of mission at the Lambeth Conference of 1988 has led me to incorporate point 5.

There is at least a possibility that this set of core values (or something very like it) might form a common set of principles around which traditional parish churches might shape and develop their life and which may also form a values template for fresh expressions of church which are part of the life of the Church of England.

I look forward to further dialogue as the journey of mission continues.

Notes

Chapter 1   Many rooms in my Father's house

1. A longer version of this essay was originally published in S. Coleman and P. Collins, *Religion, Identity and Change*, Ashgate, 2004.
2. Published by the Bedfordshire Historical Records Society, no. 69.

Chapter 2   On the analyst's couch

1. D. Davies, 'Christianity', in Jean Holm and John Bowker (eds), *Sacred Place*, Pinker, 1994.
2. Grace Davie, chapter 3, this book.
3. Church schools are sought after by parents for the excellent education and moral community they provide. Sadly they do not always positively influence young people's attitudes towards Christianity (W. K. Kay and L. J. Francis, *Drift from the Churches: Attitudes towards Christianity during Childhood and Adolescence*, University of Wales Press, 1996), another example of the generosity of the parish system, which gives out but gets little in return.
4. S. Moscovici and E. Lage, 'Studies in Social Influence II: Majorty vs minority influence in a group', *European Journal of Social Psychology*, 6, 1976, pp. 149–74.
5. F. Watts and M. Williams, *The Psychology of Religious Knowing*, Geoffrey Chapman, 1998, p. 51.
6. D. Clutterbuck and S. Kernaghan, *The Power of Empowerment*, Kogan Page, 1994.
7. A. Giddens, *Modernity and Self-identity: Self and society in the late modern age*, Polity Press, 1991.
8. E. Storkey, *The Search for Intimacy*, Hodder & Stoughton, 1995.
9. S. Savage, S. Mayo-Collins and B. Mayo, *Making Sense of Generation Y*, Church House Publishing, 2006.
10. F. Watts, R. Nye and S. Savage, *Psychology for Christian Ministry*, Routledge, 2002.
11. R. H. Kilman and W. Thomas, 'Developing a forced-choice measure of conflict handling behaviour: The MODE instrument', *Educational Psychological Measurement* 37, 1977, pp. 309–25.

12. O. F. Kernberg, *Borderline Conditions and Pathological Narcissism*, Jason Aronson, 1975.

13. A.-M. Rizutto, *The Birth of the Living God: A psychoanalytic study*, Chicago University Press, 1979.

14. A. Ellis, *Reason and Emotion in Psychotherapy*, Lyle Stewart, 1962.

15. 15 Beta, developed by the Psychology and Christianity Project at the University of Cambridge, is a ten-week multi-media adult education course interweaving psychological and biblical perspectives. For more information, please see: www.beta-course.org

16. Blackmon cited by H. N. Malony and R. Hunt, *The Psychology of Clergy*, Morehouse Publishing, 1991.

17. Maloney and Hunt, *The Psychology of Clergy*.

18. L. Francis and P. Richter, *Gone But Not Forgotten: Church leaving and returning*, Darton, Longman & Todd, 1998.

19. J. Davey, *Burnt Out: Stress in the ministry*, Gracewing, 1995.

20. S. Savage, 'Psychology serving the Church in the UK', *Journal of Psychology and Christianity*, special issue: *Psychology Collaborating with the Church*, Vol. 22: 4, 2003, pp. 338–42.

Chapter 3   From obligation to consumption

1. The following material draws extensively, though not exclusively, on my own writing. With this in mind, it should be read against the data and arguments set out in Davie, *Religion in Britain since 1945: Believing without belonging*, Blackwell, 1994, an account of the British case (a new edition is planned for 2007), and Davie, *Religion in Modern Europe: A memory mutates*, Oxford University Press, 2000 and *Europe: The Exceptional Case: Parameters of faith in the modern world*, Darton, Longman & Todd, 2002, both of which are concerned with Western Europe. Bearing this sequence of publications in mind, a second point immediately becomes clear – namely the continuing evolution in my own thinking about the religious life of this part of the world. No analysis is fixed once and for all.

2. The statistics from the original books (see n.1 for details of these publications) are not reproduced in this relatively short chapter.

3. A reputation which is not entirely justified (see the section in this chapter on vicarious religion for a fuller discussion of this point).

4. Information about the European Values Study can be found on the following website which is regularly updated: www.europeanvalues.nl. It is a useful source of information.

5. D. Voas and A. Crockett, 'Religion in Britain: neither believing nor belonging', *Sociology*, 39/1, 2005, pp. 11–12.

6. Much of the debate concerns the manner in which the terms 'believing' and

'belonging' are operationalized; if this is done too severely the original meaning of the phrase is distorted.

7. See R. Putnam, *Bowling Alone: The collapse and revival of American community*, Simon & Schuster, 2000, for a full discussion of the point.

8. See note 4 above.

9. P. Bréchon, 'L'évolution du religieux', *Futuribles*, 260, January, 2001, pp. 39–48; Y. Lambert, 'Religion: l'Europe à un tourant', *Futuribles*, 277, January–August, 2002, pp. 129–60.

10. Davie, *Religion in Modern Europe* and 'The persistence of institutional religion in modern Europe', in L. Woodhead with P. Heelas and D. Martin (eds), *Peter Berger and the Study of Religion*, Routledge, 2001, pp. 101–11.

11. Each of these is discussed in some detail in Davie, 'Vicarious religion: A methodological challenge', in N. Ammerman (ed.), *Religion in Modern Lives*, Oxford University Press, forthcoming.

12. One commentator, Anders Bäckström, put this point even more subtly: what Swedish people in fact believe in is belonging. A. Greeley (*Religion in Europe at the End of the Second Millennium*, Transaction Publishers, 2004) argues in a rather similar way with reference to Norway, rather than Sweden.

13. There is no church tax in England, but a very similar feeling that the Church exists for the benefit of the population as a whole. In this as in many other ways, the Church of England is a close cousin rather than a sibling to the state churches of Northern Europe.

14. Had Princess Diana's Muslim partner not died in the crash, the situation would have been very different. We can only speculate about the possible liturgical outcomes.

15. Paradoxically, it is in *abnormal* circumstances that *abnormal* behaviour becomes *normal*.

16. Davie, *Religion in Modern Europe*, pp. 71–8.

17. Davie, *Religion in Modern Europe*.

18. Interestingly, however, explaining 'vicariousness' to an American audience has become easier since 9/11 – an event in which the implicit most certainly became explicit (N. Ammerman, 'Grieving together: September 11 as a measure of social capital in the US', in I. Markham and I. Abu-Rabi (eds), *September 11 2001: Religious prespectives on the causes and consequences*, Oneworld Publications, 2002, pp. 53–73).

19. In this respect I largely agree with Voas and Crockett that 'believing without belonging' might 'enter honourable retirement' ('Religion in Britain', p. 25). I doubt, however, that it will be allowed to do (not least for onomatopoeic reasons). It will, I fear, continue to be abused as well as used in the debates that emerge in the twenty-first century.

20. For more information about the Kendal project, see: www.lancs.ac.uk/depts/

iepp/kendal/book.htm; and P. Heelas, and L. Woodhead, *The Spiritual Revolution: Why religion is giving way to spirituality*, Blackwell, 2005.

21. See S. Hunt, *The Alpha Enterprise: Evangelism in a post-Christian era*, Ashgate, 2004, for a very fair account of Alpha.

22. Not least S. Bruce, *Choice and Religion: A critique of rational choice and theory*, Oxford University Press, 1999; *God is Dead*, Blackwell, 2002.

Chapter 5 Focusing church life on a theology of mission

1. Michael Nazir-Ali, *Shapes of the Church to Come*, Kingsway, 2001.

2. Stuart Murray, *Church After Christendom*, Paternoster, 2004, p. 122.

3. See Paul Bayes, *Mission-shaped Church – Missionary Values, Church Planting and Fresh Expressions of Church*, Grove Books, Evangelism 67.

4. *Mission-shaped Church*, pp. 81–2.

5. For a more substantial attempt to outline the DNA of the church see Howard Snyder, *Decoding the Church*, Baker, 2002.

6. Malcolm Brown in *A Measure for Measures: In Mission and Ministry*, Church House Publishing, 2005, Appendix 1, p. 112.

7. *Mission-shaped Church*, pp. 87–92.

8. See in T. J. Gorringe, *Furthering Humanity*, Ashgate, 2004, ch. 9; Lamin Sanneh, *Translating the Message*, Orbis, 1989; Aylward Shorter, *Towards a Theology of 'Inculturation'*, Chapman, 1988; Andrew Walls, *The Cross-Cultural Process in Christian History*, T&T Clark, 2002.

9. Pedro Casaldaliga quoted in Gorringe, *Furthering Humanity*, p. 175.

10. *Mission-shaped Church*, p. 91.

11. Tex Sample, *The Spectacle of Worship in a Wired World*, Abingdon, 1998, p. 105.

12. John V. Taylor quoted in Charles H. Kraft, *Christianity in Culture*, Orbis, 1979, p. 279.

13. Paul Avis, *The Anglican Understanding of the Church*, SPCK, 2000, p. 65.

14. Richard Bauckham and Trevor Hart, *Hope Against Hope*, T&T Clark, 1999, pp. 70f.

15. Doctrine Commission, *We Believe in the Holy Spirit*, Church House Publishing, 1991, p. 173.

16. *We Believe in the Holy Spirit*, p. 171.

17. *Mission-shaped Church*, p. xiii.

18. A. Bittlinger, *Gifts and Graces*, Hodder & Stoughton, 1967.

19. Jürgen Moltmann, *Humanity in God*, SCM Press, 1983, p. 64.

20. Andrew Walls, *The Cross-Cultural Process in Christian History*, T&T Clark, 2002, p. 79.

Chapter 6 Serving, sustaining, connecting

1. *Mission-shaped Church*, pp. 36–7. This figure comprises the 10 per cent of the population who worship regularly; 10 per cent who worship occasionally and 20 per cent of people with a church background who are open to returning. The figures are based on a telephone poll of over 3,000 people conducted in the Greater London area in 1995 for Philip Richter and Leslie Francis and published in their study, *Gone But Not Forgotten* (Darton, Longman & Todd, 1998). The published Francis and Richter research was later augmented by additional telephone surveys in Devon and York.

2. A survey by Tearfund in 2004 of 5,000 adults by face to face interview and based around similar questions to the Francis and Richter research establishes similar proportions in terms of regular and occasional church worship and the proportion of the population who have no church background at all. That part of the population which is able to connect with the traditional church is a slowly diminishing proportion. Tearfund plan to track these changes annually over the coming years. The research is not yet published.

3. Even *Mission-shaped Church* is not exempt from this trend. See for example the recommendations on pp.147–8.

4. This is true not only of business and commercial contexts but of the public sector institutions. Schools, universities, the health service and the voluntary sector have all established leadership institutes of different kinds in the last decade.

5. Ephesians 4.11 must be read alongside 2.22: 'built upon the foundation of the apostles and prophets with Christ Jesus himself as the cornerstone.' This seems to be a retrospective verse with a restrictive understanding of the terms similar to the usage in Acts and a stage on from the wider designation of apostles in, for example, Romans 16.7.

6. *Ministry in Three Dimensions*, Darton, Longman & Todd, 1999.

7. Published in *Focus on Leadership*, Foundation for Church Leadership, 2005.

8. N. D. Collins, *Diakonia: reinterpreting the ancient sources*, Oxford University Press, 1990 and *Deacons and the Church: making connections old and new*, Gracewing, 2002.

9. *For Such a Time as This: a renewed diaconate in the Church of England*, GS1407, Church House Publishing, 2001. The report contains a helpful summary of Collin's ideas on pp.39ff.

10. So for example Phoebe in Romans 16.1 and Tychicus in Ephesians 4.21

11. *Common Worship Ordination of Deacons*: www.cofe.anglican.org/worship/liturgy/commonworship/texts/ordinal/deacons.html

12. The terms have been used interchangeably in the recent Anglican Ordinals with priests as the preferred term. The evolution of the English term priest is complex. Different strands of theological understanding connect the New Testament notion of the presbyter – or elder – with the Old Testament

understanding of the sacrificial priesthood (an entirely different word in Greek and Hebrew). The linkage is made in the New Testament itself through the priesthood (in the Old Testament sense) of Christ and of all God's people and this is connected with Christian ministry in Romans. Some of the patristic writers develop this understanding of sacrificial priesthood more explicitly connecting it first to the bishop and then to the presbyter. See *Ministry in Three Dimensions*, pp.100ff. for a fuller discussion.

13. For a fuller exposition of these four areas see 'Leadership in the Christian tradition' in *Focus for Leadership*, cited in n. 6 above.

Chapter 8   Good practice is not what it used to be

1. There is also the highly complex question as to what constitutes 'good practice'.
2. The Fresh Expressions team are grateful to Paul Whiffen, formerly of Knoco Ltd for presenting a version of this at their retreat in September 2005.
3. Etienne Wenger, Richard McDermott and William M. Snyder, *Cultivating Communities of Practice*, Harvard Business School, 2002, pp. 49–64.
4. It is worth emphasizing that certain forms of tacit and context-specific knowledge cannot be codified, and that they are more likely to be accessed through the 'connect' approach. See for example Ash Amin and Patrick Cohendet, *Architectures of Knowledge*, Oxford University Press, 2004, pp. 19–25.
5. An introduction to some of these tools in a business context can be found in Chris Collison and Geoff Parcell, *Learning to Fly*, Capstone, 2004.
6. I am grateful to Nick Milton of Knoco Ltd for pointing this out.
7. 'Changing values (2): Work and Leisure', 2 July 2003, www.mori.com/digest/2003.
8. Edmund King and David Leibling, 'Commuting and travel choices': www.racfoundation.org/our_research/Commutepaper.
9. Office for National Statistics, *Social Trends*, 2006, p. 208.
10. Danny Dorling and Phil Rees, 'A nation still dividing: the British census and social polarization 1971–2001', *Environment and Planning*, 35, 2003.

Chapter 9   Mapping the mixed economy

1. Some of the ideas presented in this chapter were first expounded in my book *Journeying Out*, Morehouse, 2004. This concise paper presents further insights, however, for a full expression of the arguments underpinning this threefold map readers are referred to the last four chapters in *Journeying Out*.
2. The spell that has been cast by the Enlightenment over north European minds means that African Christians look on bemused at the lack of faith, not just of

non-Christians, but of Christians in Europe. From an African perspective this lack of faith is the root of the failure of the churches' mission in Britain. However, what is less understood is the catastrophic impact that the Enlightenment emphasis on rationality has on faith. The impact of the Enlightenment is not something that can be just 'willed' away. Rather a therapeutic strategy has to be adopted to re-kindle the traces of ultimacy that remain.

3. Samuel Huntington, *The Clash of Civilizations*, Free Press, 2002.
4. See 'From obligation to consumption: Understanding the patterns of religion in Northern Europe' by Grace Davie in this volume.
5. See my book *Beyond the Good Samaritan*, Continuum, 1997, for an example of apt liturgy that takes place in a minibus.
6. It is worth noting that 'church' is an event before it is an organization or institution.
7. A cairn is a pile of stones used as a route marker to the summit of a mountain.
8. Karl Rahner, *Theological Investigations*, XI, Danton, Longman and Todd, 1974.
9. Karl W. Deutsch, *The Nerves of Government*, Free Press of Glencoe, 1963, p. 230.
10. I would make the case that holistic mission can only be achieved by an oblique route because when addressed head-on holistic mission is reduced to a sequential approach, either with evangelism being prior to social engagement of social engagement being undertaken prior to evangelism. For a fuller discussion of this see *Journeying Out*, pp. 11–18.
11. Stanley Saunders and Charles Campbell, *The Word on the Street*, Eerdmans, 2000, pp. 2–3.
12. Joseph Pine and James H. Gilmore, *The Experience Economy*, Harvard Business School Press, 1999, p. ix (italics in original).
13. More simply put, Camden is a trendy place with lots of different styles, visit Camden Lock and see and be seen . . . and spend!
14. Pine and Gilmore, *The Experience Economy*, p. 165.
15. *The Experience Economy*, p. 190.
16. Richard Sennett, *The Fall of Public Man*, Penguin Books, 2003, p. 56.

Chapter 10 Fresh expressions growing to maturity

1. The phrase entered our vocabulary through the speech of Archbishop Rowan Williams at the General Synod debate on *Mission-shaped Church* in February 2004.
2. See the overall progression within Stephen Covey, *Seven Habits of Highly Effective People*, Simon & Schuster, 1989.
3. Cf. the title of Robert Warren's *Being Human Being Church*, Church House Publishing, 1995.

4. Ireneaus, *Adversus Haereses* IV, 20.7.
5. David Watson, *I Believe in the Church*, Hodder, 1978, chapter 19.
6. This is the gist of the approach taken by Archbishop Rowan Williams speaking to the Church of England's church planters in June 2004.
7. See Paul Avis, *The Anglican Understanding of the Church*, SPCK, 2000, p. 9.
8. *Mission-shaped Church*, Church House Publishing, 2004, p. 99.
9. This is the reproach contained in chapter 8 of Vincent Donovan's *Christianity Rediscovered*, SCM Press, 2001.
10. *Mission-shaped Church*, p. 93.
11. The introduction to the 1989 report *Patterns of Worship* is the most cogent case against this instinct.

Chapter 11   Reconfiguring a diocese towards mission

1. Bob Jackson, *Hope for the Church*, Church House Publishing, 2002; *The Road to Growth*, Church House Publishing, 2005.
2. *Hope for the Church*, pp. 169f.
3. *The Road to Growth*, p. 80.
4. Gordon Kuhrt (ed.), *Ministry Issues for the Church of England*, Church House Publishing, 2001, pp, 77, 78.
5. *Review of Clergy Terms of Service 1 and 2*, Church House Publishing, 2004 and 2005.
6. *A Measure for Measures, in Mission and Ministry*, Church House Publishing, 2004.
7. The Diocesan Strategy 1999–2004, p. 20.
8. L. Paul, *The Deployment and Payment of the Clergy*, CIO, 1964.
9. Michael Turnbull, 'The parish system' in Kuhrt, *Ministry Issues*, p. 213.
10. Robert Warren and Janet Hodgson, *Growing Healthy Churches*, Springboard, 2001.
11. Turnbull in Kuhrt, *Ministry Issues*, pp. 213–14.
12. Paul Avis, *The Anglican Understanding of the Church*, SPCK, 2000, pp. 15ff.
13. See Jackson, *The Road to Growth*, ch. 14f.
14. John Tiller, *A Strategy for the Church's Ministry*, Church Information Office, 1983.
15. Jackson, *The Road to Growth*, pp. 101f., 124ff.
16. See I. Cundy and J. Welby in G. E. Evans and M. Percy (eds), *Managing the Church?: Order and organization in a secular age*, Sheffield Academic Press, 2000, pp. 42ff.
17. Paul Bayes, *Mission-shaped Church – Missionary Values, Church Planting and Fresh Expressions of Church*, Grove Books, Evangelism 67, p. 23.
18. *Working as One Body*, Church House Publishing, 1995.
19. See Jackson, *The Road to Growth*, ch. 14.

20. Jackson, *Hope for the Church*, p. 181.
21. See, Jackson, *Hope for the Church*, p. 182, where the 'seven marks of a healthy church' are set out, or Warren and Hodgson, *Growing Healthy Churches.*

Chapter 12   Legal matters – what you need to know

1. Much time was taken up in the Church Assembly after World War II in providing a new body of Canons, to replace the Canons of 1603, and the essential structures of the present Pastoral Measure (consolidated in 1983) were laid in the Pastoral Measure 1967, in the same year as the Extra-Parochial Ministry Measure was passed (as to which, see above, page 174).
2. One diocesan pastoral secretary is reported as having said he had never (in ten years) been shown a copy of the Pastoral Measure 1983, and had been told it was out of print.
3. The Decade of Evangelism had sprung out of a decision of the Lambeth Conference in 1988 Lambeth Conference 1988, Resolution 43. For a mid-90s assessment of the impact of the Decade of Evangelism across the Anglican Communion, see Okorocha (ed.), *The Cutting Edge of Mission*, Anglican Communion Publications, 1996.
4. Board of Mission, *Setting the Agenda and Beyond*, Occasional Paper 10, Church House Publishing, 1999.
5. *Setting the Agenda*, pp. 97, 98.
6. In Halsbury's *Statutes*, fourth ed., vol. 14.
7. *A Measure for Measures*, GS 1528, Church House Publishing, 2004.
8. *Mission-shaped Church*, GS 1523, Church House Publishing, 2004.
9. Which will be brought forward in two stages, the first dealing with the major changes, and the second a consolidation of those changes with the existing 1983 material, to create one composite Measure.
10. Section I sets the tone: 'It shall be the duty of any person or body carrying out functions under this Measure ... to have due regard to the mission of the Church of England.'
11. Part V, clauses 47–51 of the draft Measure (GS 1597A).
12. Clause 47(1).
13. Clause 47(5):
    'Any bishops' mission order may include provision –
    (a) for participation in a local ecumenical project (commonly known as a "local ecumenical partnership"),
    (b) for other ecumenical cooperation with other Churches, and
    (c) for collaboration with any religious organizations,
    and in this section and sections 48 to 50 below any provision mentioned in this subsection is referred to as "cooperation provision".'
14. Clause 47(4).
15. The draft legislation envisages projects in which large numbers may be

affected, going beyond a single deanery, or in some cases a single diocese (see Clause 47(11)).

16. Clause 47(15).
17. Clause 51; the Code is to have the endorsement of the General Synod before it comes into force, but once in force 'any leader, any Visitor and any pastoral committee shall be under a duty to have regard to [it]' – (Clause 51(5)).
18. Clause 48 sets out the Visitor's role in some detail.
19. No doubt because of the Nine o'clock Service debacle in 1995, but also because of the charity law difficulties which arise if initiatives of this sort become detached from their denominational sponsorship, as has happened on a number of occasions with 'church plants' and other similar initiatives.
20. See Canon C 18.1, 18.4.
21. Clause 50(5)(b).
22. Clause 50(7)(b).
23. The Measure can be found in Halsbury, *Statutes* (see n. 6 above); on the General Synod website and on the HMSO website.
24. The legal authority for Conventional Districts is generally taken to be a reference in the definition of 'parish' in *Church Representation Rules* 54(1)
25. Extra-Parochial Ministry Measure, s.21(1).
26. See above p. 173.
27. The base need not be permanent, or held under freehold tenure – see Opinion of the Legal Advisory Commission obtained specifically on the point [revised edition to be published later in 2006].
28. And if a 'church' is a community which 'rightly and duly administers the sacraments' as well as proclaiming the Word of God, can a 'virtual' Christian community ever be a 'church'?

Conclusion

1. To proclaim the good news of the kingdom; to teach, nurture and baptize new believers; to respond to human need by loving service; to seek to transform unjust structures of society; to strive to safeguard the integrity of creation and sustain and renew the earth.

General index